Claude Bernard

Michael Foster

BIBLIOBAZAAR

Copyright © BiblioBazaar, LLC

BiblioBazaar Reproduction Series: Our goal at BiblioBazaar is to help readers, educators and researchers by bringing back in print hard-to-find original publications at a reasonable price and, at the same time, preserve the legacy of literary history. The following book represents an authentic reproduction of the text as printed by the original publisher and may contain prior copyright references. While we have attempted to accurately maintain the integrity of the original work(s), from time to time there are problems with the original book scan that may result in minor errors in the reproduction, including imperfections such as missing and blurred pages, poor pictures, markings and other reproduction issues beyond our control. Because this work is culturally important, we have made it available as a part of our commitment to protecting, preserving and promoting the world's literature.

All of our books are in the "public domain" and many are derived from Open Source projects dedicated to digitizing historic literature. We believe that when we undertake the difficult task of re-creating them as attractive, readable and affordable books, we further the mutual goal of sharing these works with a larger audience. A portion of Bibliobazaar profits go back to Open Source projects in the form of a donation to the groups that do this important work around the world. If you would like to make a donation to these worthy Open Source projects, or would just like to get more information about these important initiatives, please visit www.bibliobazaar.com/opensource.

CLAUDE BERNARD.

CLAUDE BERNARD

BY

MICHAEL FOSTER, M.A., M.D., D.C.L., Etc.

Secretary of the Royal Society of London

PROFESSOR OF PHYSIOLOGY IN THE UNIVERSITY OF CAMBRIDGE

NEW YORK
LONGMANS, GREEN & CO.
91 & 93, FIFTH AVENUE
1899

Dedication.

TO THE PHYSIOLOGISTS OF FRANCE,

BOTH TO THOSE WHO HAD THE HAPPINESS TO KNOW

CLAUDE BERNARD IN THE FLESH, AND TO THOSE WHO,

LIKE MYSELF, NEVER SAW HIS FACE, THIS LITTLE

SKETCH IS DEDICATED IN THE HOPE THAT

AS HE HAS BEEN TO ME A FATHER IN

OUR COMMON SCIENCE, SO I MAY

BE ALLOWED TO LOOK UPON

THEM AS BRETHREN.

M. FOSTER.

PREFACE

SOME may think that in the pages which follow too much space is given to an exposition of Claude Bernard's scientific work and too little to the details of his life as a man. Although the real life of every great man of science lies in the story of his scientific work and not in the tale of how he passed his days, we all of us wish to clothe the image which we have formed of a man whom we know by his writings only, with as many details as we can gather, of how he moved among his fellow-men, and what befell him on

PREFACE

his path through life. And had I been able to do so, I would have added much to what I have written. But the details which can now be gained of Bernard's daily life are very scanty. I can only say that I have done my best ; and the little which I have been able to do has been made possible by the kindness of my friends, especially of Prof. A. Dastre, who now holds Bernard's chair at the Sorbonne ; of Prof. C. Richet, of the École de Médecine ; and of Prof. W. Kühne, of Heidelberg, who was once Bernard's pupil.

CAMBRIDGE,
May 3, 1899.

CONTENTS

		PAGE
I.	EARLY DAYS	1
II.	THE CONDITION OF PHYSIOLOGICAL SCIENCE BEFORE BERNARD BEGAN HIS LABOURS	22
III.	EARLY LABOURS	43
IV.	GLYCOGEN	61
V.	VASO-MOTOR NERVES	100
VI.	OTHER DISCOVERIES	135
VII.	HIS LATER WRITINGS	160
VIII.	LATER YEARS	198
IX.	CONCLUSION	226
INDEX		239

CLAUDE BERNARD

I

EARLY DAYS

THE traveller speeding southwards by the Paris, Lyons and Mediterranean express, some little time before he reaches Lyons rushes through the station belonging to the town of Villefranche. Not far from that town—two or three leagues distant—lies the little village of Saint-Julien (Rhône), in which on July 12, 1813, Claude Bernard was born. His father was, in common with most of his neighbours, the humble proprietor of a

CLAUDE BERNARD

small estate chiefly planted with vines, and derived at least most of his income from making wine. The whole district was, and indeed still is, a wine-producing land ; it is part of the old province of Beaujolais, and the wine which it yields bears that name.

The little estate eventually came into Bernard's hands, and so soon as he could afford it, or at least in his later years, he used the paternal cottage as a summer residence during the vacations. Here he yearly renewed his strength by touch with his native earth, exchanging Paris for the simplicities of country life, and mingling quiet literary labours with the amusement of watching the vintage of his own wine. He thus himself describes his home :

"My dwelling is on the hill slopes of Beaujolais which look towards the Dombe. The Alps give me my horizon and when

EARLY DAYS

the air is clear I can catch sight of their white summits. At the same time I see spread out before me for two leagues the prairies of the Saône. The slope on which I dwell is surrounded on all sides by vineyards stretching away apparently without limit; these would give the country a monotonous appearance were not this broken by wooded valleys and brooks running down from the mountains to the river. My cottage, situated though it is on a rise, is a very nest of verdure, thanks to a little wood which shades it on the right and to an orchard which flanks it on the left; a great rarity in a land in which they stub up even the coppices in order to plant vines."

In this quiet, out-of-the-way spot, the future physiologist began life as a member of a homely family, whose aspirations scarcely went beyond securing their daily bread. As a child he must have been bright, for the curé took him under his special charge, making him a choir boy and teaching him Latin. He afterwards was sent to the school or so-called college at Villefranche, directed by the Jesuits.

When he had learnt as much as his teachers could teach him at the college, he was sent to Lyons, with the view probably, in the first instance, of his completing his studies and obtaining the Baccalauréat. But his student career at Lyons could not have been a very lengthy one, for he soon entered into active life, exchanging the school for the shop. The reasons which led to this step cannot be ascertained, but they do seem to have been financial. The family, though humble, were not without resources. Claude appears to have been an only son, with one sister, who

EARLY DAYS

eventually married a neighbouring proprietor. The father seems to have been still alive (though he is said to have died while Bernard was yet young) and not yet to have met with the reverses which subsequently crippled the family. Be it as it may, Bernard, somewhere in his teens, became engaged at Lyons in practical pharmacy, having obtained a situation with a pharmacist in the Faubourg de Vaise of that city. He received at first nothing more than his board and lodging for his services in the shop, though after some months, his manual dexterity, shown by the singular neatness of his "dispensing," was rewarded by a humble salary.

Here for some time, probably for two years, Bernard spent most of his days as a pharmaceutical assistant, dispensing medicines, and carrying them to the clients, especially to the Veterinary School. What

CLAUDE BERNARD

opportunities for pharmaceutical study he had does not appear; but his patron's mode of conducting his business served to awake in him early the spirit of medical scepticism. As was usual at that epoch the clients of the shop, especially the old women of the outlying villages, made a constant demand for a syrup which seemed to cure everything; and Bernard, to his astonishment, found that this favourite syrup was compounded of all the spoilt drugs and remnants of the shop. Whenever Bernard reported that a bottle of stuff had gone wrong, "Keep that for syrup," replied the master; "that will do for making the syrup."

No wonder that Bernard's mind turned with avidity to other things than pharmacy. In common with many of the young men of his time, he was filled with literary aspirations; and he was particularly drawn

EARLY DAYS

towards the dramatic art. All his free evenings he spent at the play, at the Théâtre des Célestins, and was moved to write himself a vaudeville comedy, entitled "La Rose du Rhône," which was not only accepted, but had a certain success on the boards, though it was never printed.

Encouraged by the result of this first effort, he set himself to the serious work of writing a historic piece in the conventional five acts, giving it at first the form of a tragedy in metre, but subsequently changing it to a prose drama. With this he determined to seek his fortune in Paris. He had in Lyons two friends, like himself, students and poor. All three thought that Lyons was too small a sphere for their abilities, all three determined that the proper place for them was Paris. They parted from each other at Lyons, giving each other the rendezvous

CLAUDE BERNARD

in Paris, or as they called it, " la scène du Monde." And Bernard used to tell afterwards, in a joking spirit, how by chance they did later on meet together in the Place du Panthéon, in front of the well-known inscription " Aux grands Hommes la Patrie reconnaissante " ! And though the omen did not hold so good for the other two as it did for Bernard, yet one became a Bishop, and the other a Director of Railways.

Bernard, with the help of the few francs which his little comedy had put in his pocket, started in the diligence for Paris, armed with his manuscript of " Arthur de Bretagne," carefully rolled up, and with a letter of introduction to the great critic Saint-Marc Girardin, which a professor in the Faculty of Letters at Lyons had given him. It was in 1834, and he was just about one and twenty years old.

EARLY DAYS

Girardin, then Professor at the Sorbonne, received the young student kindly, and conscientiously read his manuscript. He saw (as indeed one may see now, for the drama was published in a fine edition after Bernard's death in 1886, by the Librairie Dentu of Paris), that the drama showed that the author possessed literary powers of no mean kind; but he shrank from giving to the aspirant the hopes which might have been his due. Instead of encouraging him to devote himself to literature he bade him turn to something else by which to earn his bread, and court the Muses in his leisure moments only. "You have studied pharmacy," said he; "study medicine, you will thereby much more surely gain a livelihood."

Bernard followed the advice, and threw himself heart and soul into medical studies, living in the most frugal manner, supporting himself and paying the necessary fees chiefly with the scant money which he earned by giving lessons ; for his family could spare him very little help, at most some trifling sums of money and an occasional hamper of country produce. Moreover his father died about this time, having met with reverses before his death. But a student's life in the Quartier Latin, at that time at all events, was not a costly affair. A garret, shared perhaps by a comrade, served as bedroom and study, and at times as kitchen, for when a gift came from the country home it was cooked and eaten in the "appartement," with the help of utensils impressed or borrowed from the laboratory.

Bernard worked hard at all his medical studies, and in the tumult of the new ideas crowding in upon him his old literary aspirations soon grew faint and vanished.

EARLY DAYS

Most especially did he devote himself to anatomy and physiology. In the former he recognised a branch of science, limited it is true in range, but one which had been studied with such rigour and exactitude as to have become a mental discipline of no mean value. He soon made himself master of the subject, acquiring a knowledge of it at once extensive and minute, while his conspicuous manual dexterity led to the dissections which he made being regarded by others as anatomical preparations of singular completeness and value. Moreover, he seems in these early days to have looked forward to the career of a surgeon as the one by which he might hope to gain a livelihood; and to such a career anatomy was the most direct path. Physiology was at that time in a very different condition from anatomy; in place of light there was for the most part darkness, and in place of clear and distinct guidance, uncertainty and dubious discussion. What Bernard thought of the most of the teaching of physiology of the time, we can gather from his utterances later on; and we can confidently suppose that even in his early days he clearly distinguished between the science as it was taught and the science as it ought to be taught. If anatomy served to supply his intellectual appetite for exact and minute knowledge in the shape of concrete facts, physiology served to awaken in his mind the desire to solve problems by a direct experimental appeal to nature. He lived as a student in the Quartier Latin in a little "entresol" in the old "Passage du Commerce Saint André des Arts," not far from the spot where Marat printed "L'Ami du Peuple," from the house in which Danton lived, and from that in which

EARLY DAYS

Guillotin tried the value of his famous invention on the necks of sheep. In that little apartment he made his first attempts at experiments on living animals. A little later on he, in partnership with a fellow student, Lasègue, opened a humble experimental laboratory in the old Rue Saint-Jacques, nearly opposite the Collége de France, his purpose in doing so being, apparently, partly to gain some money by fees, but partly, and perhaps chiefly, to obtain ampler and more convenient means for carrying on his own budding researches. Alas, the enterprise was not successful. Only some half-dozen students availed themselves of the opportunity offered. The fees never brought enough to pay the rent and the cost of the rabbits employed, and the little laboratory was soon closed.

Nor in his more strictly professional

CLAUDE BERNARD

efforts did Bernard at first attract attention. Retiring, thoughtful, with his mind already bent on problems to be solved, awkward in manner, and wholly removed from the desire so common to others to appear better than he really was, he did not impress either his comrades or the authorities with his power.

To the former, indeed, except in the dissecting-room, he appeared somewhat idle and inattentive. They were for the most part unable to criticise their teachers. Their intellectual activity was chiefly receptive; it rarely went beyond the task of carefully listening to the words which fell from the professorial chair, and treasuring them in their memories to be reproduced at ,the appointed time in the examination room. He, on the contrary, seems to have begun early to ponder over the questions which were treated of in the

EARLY DAYS

lectures ; he soon detected flaws in his teachers' reasoning, and thus speedily beginning to doubt the value of the teaching, paid but a listless attention to expositions and discussions, the weakness of which became more and more clear to him as time went on. Such a spirit, though it may bear admirable fruit in the end, is not very profitable at the schools. Possibly, moreover, the young student, quiet and reserved as he seemed, had within him not a little intellectual pride, which tempted him to neglect beyond measure instruction which seemed to him of dubious value. Though in his examinations and otherwise he showed himself to be an able student, neither to his fellow students nor to his teachers did he seem one who was about to make a great mark.

In the fifth year of his studies, however,

CLAUDE BERNARD

his opportunity came to him. After serving as usual as "externe" at the Hospitals he was in 1839 appointed "interne"; and Providence ruled that he should be allotted to Magendie, who was then one of the Physicians to the Hôtel Dieu.

Magendie, then the leading physiologist in France, held two offices. He was Physician to the Hôtel Dieu, and Professor of Medicine at the Collége de France.

The latter famous institution was founded by Francis I. in 1530, the year after the Treaty of Cambray, under the name of the *Collége Royal* or *Collége des trois langues*, the first chairs established being those of Greek, Hebrew, and Latin. It was founded as a place of free learning with the desire to antagonise the more rigid and scholastic teaching of the University in the Sorbonne. The Royal Readers or Professors paid directly by the King were free to teach as

EARLY DAYS

they pleased within the subjects defined by their titles. The lectures were open to all without fees, and the whole object of the foundation was to encourage liberal and higher learning. At first the College had no fixed abode, the Professors delivering their lectures where they could ; indeed it was not until 1610 that Louis XIII., carrying out the promise made by Henry IV., began the construction of a building which, however, through various delays, was not completed and hence not used until 1636.

To the chairs of the three tongues, Francis I. added those of mathematics, philosophy, and medicine, the first holder of that of medicine being the Florentine Guido Guidi, known as Vidus Vidius, who entered into the post in 1542. He was succeeded in 1550 by the great anatomist Jacques du Bois, better known by his Latin

CLAUDE BERNARD

name of Jacobus Sylvius, one Beauvais intervening for three years.

Various other chairs were subsequently founded, and in the course of time numerous changes took place. Charles IX. founded in 1568 a chair of medicine, Henry III. founded one of surgery in 1575, and Henry IV. in 1595 one of anatomy, botany, and pharmacy, the second holder of which was Jean Riolan. By 1680, all these four chairs had come to be all equally devoted to medicine, surgery, botany, and pharmacy.

Towards the close of the eighteenth century, however, great changes were made. The first chair of medicine became a chair of chemistry, held from 1865 onwards by the present eminent chemist Berthelot. The second chair of medicine became a chair of Natural History held by the illustrious Cuvier from 1799 to 1832.

EARLY DAYS

And the chair of surgery became the one chair of Medicine held for some years by Laënnec, and filled at the time of which we are speaking by Magendie.

During all these years, however, the principle of the College remained the same. The professors were at liberty to lecture without the restraints of a syllabus having an examination as its goal, the lectures were free to all who wished to hear, and the general idea that the place was devoted to higher study still maintained its sway.

Following the old tradition, it continued to be recognised that the duty of a Professor holding a chair in the College was not to give didactic lectures suitable to an ordinary student, but rather to use the post as an instrument of research, and to expound new ideas to those who were already advanced in their studies. Thus, for example, the lectures which Magendie delivered there in 1838–40 were afterwards published in the well-known work, "Phénomènes Physiques de la Vie." Carrying out the idea of research, there was allotted to the Professor of Medicine in a lower story of the building accommodation for research in the form of a dark unwholesome room called a laboratory. There was also provided for the Professor a *préparateur* to assist him in the experiments with which he illustrated his lectures, or in those connected with his researches.

Bernard's first contact with Magendie was not promising. The professor, in the ward and in the laboratory at least, was in manner abrupt, even rough and rude. He took little notice of his new *interne*, hardly even asking his name. After not many days, however, the conspicuously skilful way in which Bernard carried out

EARLY DAYS

the dissections which were entrusted to him made a very marked impression on his master; and the story goes that one day, early in their intercourse, Magendie, on a sudden, called out roughly to Bernard, busy at a dissection, "I say, you there, I take you as my *préparateur* at the Collége de France." Bernard was only too glad to accept the offer. There is some doubt as to whether he was not, during the first year, a mere voluntary assistant, but in any case, in 1841 he had become the official *préparateur*. Bernard's career as a physiologist may be said to date from then. Before proceeding any further, however, it will be desirable to form some idea of the state of physiology in Europe in general, and in France in particular at this epoch.

II

THE CONDITION OF PHYSIOLOGICAL SCIENCE BEFORE BERNARD BEGAN HIS LABOURS

WHEN the physiologist to-day, knowing how dominant has been the influence of Germany on physiology in the present century, inquires what was the condition of physiology in Germany in about the year 1840, when Bernard joined Magendie, he is at once struck with the fact that the great German physiologists of the present century, Ludwig, Helmholtz, du Bois-Reymond, and Brücke, had at that time not commenced their labours. All the great work which these have done was done after that date ; their labours were contemporaneous with those of Bernard. The dominant physiological mind in Germany at that time was that of Johannes Müller. That great man had in his earlier years devoted much time to definite physiological inquiry, especially into problems relating to the senses ; he was a great teacher of physiology, inspiring a love for the science and a true spirit of inquiry into it among his numerous pupils ; and he had written a masterly text book, his "Outlines of Physiology," the influence of which not only on his own countrymen but on others has been profound.

Johannes Müller has been called a "vitalist," and in a certain sense he was one. In his "Outlines" he criticises the views of Reil "that the phenomena of life are the result, manifestation, or property of a certain combination of elements," and

CLAUDE BERNARD

contends for the necessity of supposing the existence of an "organic or vital principle or force," " the action of which, however, is not independent of certain conditions." In judging Johannes Müller's scientific attitude, it must be remembered that though a physiologist he was also a morphologist, and indeed, on the whole, more the latter than the former; hence the organic principle was of more importance to him as a something determining the form of living beings than as an explanation of the phenomena presented by their activity. Moreover he was not a vitalist in the sense that he discouraged attempts to solve the problems offered by the actions of living beings by experiments based on the view that these were the outcome of physico-chemical agencies, or that he refused to admit a physico-chemical explanation when this could be shown to be adequately valid.

PHYSIOLOGICAL SCIENCE

He was a vitalist only in the sense that he was theoretically of opinion that even when the physico-chemical analysis of vital phenomena had been pushed as far as it could, there would still remain a large residue which could not be explained through any such analysis however complete. And indeed the fact that his pupils, the great men mentioned above, were conspicuous by their efforts to solve physiological problems by such a chemico-physical analysis, shows clearly how much the master's vitalism, so far as physiology was concerned, was academic in nature, and that his influence as a teacher was strongly in the direction of guiding the physiologist to attack his problems, by the same methods, and in the same spirit, that the chemist or the physicist attacked his.

The teaching and influence in the same direction of another great man, E.

H. Weber, was even more decided and clear ; for he by the bent of his mind, no less than by fraternal ties, was not only a physiologist, but also a physicist.

The other strong men in Germany were also teaching and practising the same view. It is only necessary to mention the names of Henle, who though in the main an anatomist, was ever in search of physiological light, of Tiedemann, of Volkmann, of Vierordt, and of Bidder, to say nothing of the earlier labours of Theodore Schwann. The mark of all these was that they set about the solution of physiological problems in the same spirit in which the physicist or chemist sets about his ; to them the canons of scientific inquiry were the same for living as for nonliving phenomena ; they only had recourse, and then with reluctance, to vitalistic

PHYSIOLOGICAL SCIENCE

explanations when their means of analysis proved impotent.

On the whole the dominant spirit of physiological inquiry in Germany was at that time very much what it is now. The contrast between to-day and then lies chiefly in the paucity of opportunity for, and in the scarcity of men engaged in, experimental inquiry. Physiological laboratories, such as abound now, were then almost unknown. But in this respect physiology was hardly in a worse condition than the other experimental sciences. Until Liebig began his career at Giessen, chemical laboratories as we now know them did not exist, and physical laboratories were a still later creation. Such things do not come until a call has been made for them. The call was being made for them and they soon came. The time at which Bernard began his work at Paris, was also the time for an

CLAUDE BERNARD

independent development in Germany of opportunities for, and of the prosecution of, physiological research ; it was then that Ludwig and the other great German physiologists began their active careers.

In England the pursuit of physiology as a distinct science had but few followers, but these for the most part were treading the experimental path. The energetic expositions by Marshall Hall of the reflex actions of the nervous system, following up and extending as they did the earlier leadings of Charles Bell, were showing that this part of physiology, apparently the farthest removed from the sciences of inorganic nature, might be successfully studied by the same experimental methods.

John Reid, by his researches on the cranial nerves, was working in a more special and narrower way towards the same end. The sagacious Sharpey was

PHYSIOLOGICAL SCIENCE

teaching and was encouraging research in a spirit identical with that which governs physiological inquiry at the present day. And in the very year 1840, up to which we have so far traced Bernard's life, William Bowman made known to the world the results of those inquiries into the structure of muscle, and was about soon to make known the results of those other inquiries into the structure of the kidney, which still remain and will always remain models of histological research so directed as to throw light on physiological problems. One man only of mark, John Goodsir, and he more a morphologist than a physiologist, was teaching views in which a mystical tendency tempted the mind away from the more commonplace paths of simple observation and experiment.

In Italy, pressed down as she was at the time by political difficulties, and bound by ecclesiastical bonds, even less was being done, though, somewhat earlier, Spallanzani and Fontana had shown what could be achieved amid such adverse influences. Matteuci and others were, it is true, carrying out valuable researches on ordinary lines; but no prominent mind was distinctly influencing general physiological thought.

Turning now to France itself we find a somewhat different condition of things. In that country, perhaps, even more than in other countries, patriotism has a tendency to manifest itself by a too exclusive attention to views put forward by native writers; and this was in some ways especially the case at the epoch with which we are dealing. The influences which, as we have just said, were becoming potent as regards physiological inquiry in Germany, and were also producing a marked effect in England, were, it would seem, felt but little in

PHYSIOLOGICAL SCIENCE

France. The Frenchman who dealt with physiological questions was in the main influenced by his predecessors in his own land. And at that time the teachings of two men were in different ways especially powerful. The influence of the great Cuvier, who had mastered not only his subject but his opponents, was at that time supreme. He, like other morphologists, impressed with the impotence of the mechanical explanations offered as solutions of morphological problems, was led to depreciate, in like manner, any physico-chemical explanation offered as a solution of a physiological problem, and so became an ardent supporter of vitalistic views. His influence was, so to speak, from the outside ; yet it was a living influence and had only ceased to be such a few years before. Within the science of physiology itself the influence of Bichat,

[margin: Cuvier view.]

CLAUDE BERNARD

though it was that of a man who had long passed away, was exceedingly powerful. Bichat had laid hold of a great idea, one which rapidly spread from the land in which it was first expounded to other lands, and has in a most marked way helped to make physiology an exact science, the idea that the life of the body is the outcome of the combined and adjusted lives of the constituent tissues. By his brilliant exposition of this fruitful idea, he had opened up new ways for an exact experimental analysis of physiological phenomena. But in the detailed application of this idea, which in the flush of his youthful enthusiasm he strove to make complete and symmetric, undertaking a task the doing of which has needed, and still needs, the continued successive labours of many inquirers, he often went astray. Moreover, he so far remained under the

PHYSIOLOGICAL SCIENCE

influence of that vitalistic teaching which, in spite of what Haller had done, was still potent in the latter part of the eighteenth century, that he based his whole exposition on the idea that vital manifestations are the result of a conflict between vital forces on the one hand and physico-chemical forces on the other; he taught that these were essentially antagonistic, and that the latter have full play only when the former vanish in death. Had he lived longer he might perhaps have freed himself from the many conceptions which lessen the value of his great work; but he was taken away too soon, for he died at the early age of 31, just about the age at which Bernard began to publish. And, as often happens, the parts of his labours which were specious and misleading appeared the most tempting to many who followed him. These dwelt more on his view of

CLAUDE BERNARD

organic sensibility and contractility to which his division into organic and animal life had led him, than on his conception that each tissue had its own life, and were more pleased with his epigrammatic definition of life as the sum of forces which resist death than with his laborious attempts to define the characters of the several tissues.

Bichat, by dividing the vital principle and distributing it over the several tissues, attributing to it different functions in different parts, in reality dealt a deathblow to the old vitalistic conceptions. But he did not live long enough to grasp the conclusion to which his labours were leading, and his successors for the most part stopped also where he himself had left off.

Vitalism was thus dominant in France, especially dominant perhaps in medical doctrines. Some indeed maintained that

PHYSIOLOGICAL SCIENCE

the phenomena of living bodies could never be the subject of exact experimental inquiry. Bernard himself states that in his earlier days he heard a professor of surgery, one Gerdy, say, "When the physiologist asserts that vital phenomena remain identical under identical conditions, he proclaims an error; such is only true of non-living bodies."

[*margin note: Quote on Vitalism*]

Within physiology itself a way was opened for the encouragement of experimental inquiry by the development of a modified vitalism which taught that the phenomena of living bodies might be divided into two classes : those which are the outcome of chemico-physical causes, and those which are not, and which can be attributed only to the action of a vital principle or force. The former may be studied by ordinary experimental methods; the latter are beyond inquiry, " their causes

CLAUDE BERNARD

mock alike our conceptions and our curiosity."[1]

Such was the scientific attitude of Magendie, who, when Bernard began his medical studies, stood far above all others, as the physiologist of France. Flourens, the showy Perpetual Secretary of the Academy of Sciences, who approached physiology rather from the side of natural science than from that of medicine, had, it is true, achieved a great reputation; but, even when we have made every allowance for his work on the semicircular canals, his influence on physiology, when carefully weighed, falls far below that which the fame he enjoyed during his lifetime indicated. Longet and others were doing praiseworthy though limited work. But Magendie was the man who, during the

[1] Magendie, "Phén. phys. de la Vie," vol. ii. p. 47.

PHYSIOLOGICAL SCIENCE

first half of the century, was justly acknowledged as the physiologist of France.

And that scientific attitude of his, to which we have just referred, was indirectly the cause of his experimental activity. Having paid his tribute to vitalism by admitting that some of the phenomena of living beings were beyond the scope of experimental investigation, he felt free to throw himself, without any restraint whatever, into the research of those phenomena which he deemed open to experiment. He became in this way the apostle of physiological experiment. While in Germany, as we have just said, researches of an experimental character were relatively rare, and rarer still in England and elsewhere, Magendie from the very commencement of his career, in 1807 or thereabouts, was unceasing in experimental investigations; he did alone with his own hand in

CLAUDE BERNARD

France as much as, or more than, was being done by others in all other lands ; and though, as we have said, the spirit of such a kind of inquiry was present both in Germany and elsewhere, and the workers in these lands had no need to go abroad to be taught the true method of inquiry, there can be no doubt that the influence of Magendie's example, as one who subjected every physiological question which he touched to the test of experiment, was felt far and wide, and passed to countries other than his own.

Magendie's contributions to physiological science were many and great ; the exact and full proof which he brought forward of the truth which Charles Bell had divined rather than demonstrated, that the anterior and posterior roots of spinal nerves have essentially different functions, a truth which is the very foundation

PHYSIOLOGICAL SCIENCE

of the physiology of the nervous system, is enough by itself to mark him as a great physiologist; and he did much else besides. But all his lasting results, even when their fullest value is allotted to them, are incommensurate with his activity. If he did many experiments which bore adequate fruit, he did also many which were misleading and many which were useless. For his worship of the experimental method came very near to being idolatry. Repelled by the sterile discussions in which the vitalists and other doctrinaires of the day spent their intellectual activity, he was driven towards the other extreme, and arrived almost at the position of substituting experiment for thinking. So far from regarding an experiment as a thing to be had recourse to as a test, by which to determine whether a view derived from observation and medi-

CLAUDE BERNARD

tation were true or no, he rather thought, or seemed by his practice and indeed his teaching to think, that an experiment was the first step towards getting light. He so to speak thrust his knife here and there, to see what would come of it. He indeed confessed, in a way, that this was the nature of his method. Speaking of himself he says, "Every one is fond of comparing himself to something great and grandiose, as Louis XIV. likened himself to the sun, and others have had like similes. I am more humble. I am a mere street scavenger (*chiffonnier*) of science. With my hook in my hand and my basket on my back, I go about the streets of science, collecting what I find."

Hence, when Bernard entered upon his post as assistant to Magendie, he found himself subject to two influences antagonistic the one to the other. On the one

PHYSIOLOGICAL SCIENCE

hand, he had to listen, especially in medical circles, to expositions of vitalistic views, to the depreciation of the experimental method as a false guide in inquiries concerning the phenomena of living beings. On the other hand, he was brought into daily touch with a man who scoffed at all theory and ridiculed reasoned discussions, and who, while he refused to apply the test of experiment to certain questions of physiology, exalted experiment in the regions in which he did apply it, to the almost complete exclusion of other means of inquiry.

In spite of the personal influences which Magendie must have exerted on him, the young assistant had the genius to strike out a path for himself. While recognising, as clearly as did his master, the value of experiment as the final test of all physiological views, he, on the one hand,

CLAUDE BERNARD

deposed experiment from its false throne, making it the servant and not the master of reasoned speculations; and, on the other hand, as we shall see, extended its domains, showing how, under proper use, it could be applied without distinction to all the phenomena of life. In doing so the pupil went far beyond the master; that which the multitude of blind experiments made by the latter have left behind as a lasting contribution to physiological science is but little compared to that which has come from the much fewer experiments of the former, guided as they were in every case by previous meditation and thought.

III

EARLY LABOURS

BY his appointment as *préparateur* to Magendie Bernard was fairly started on the career of an experimental physiologist. Outside his duties at the Collége de France, he had to devote some time to the delivery of private courses of lectures in order to eke out his slender income ; the rest he gave up to research, his investigations being carried on chiefly if not exclusively in some place or other which he had temporarily fitted up as a private laboratory, or in the chemical laboratory of one or other of his friends. There was

CLAUDE BERNARD

not room for him, it would appear, to conduct his own private work in the laboratory of the Collége de France.

In May, 1843, he published his first communication, "Recherches anatomiques et physiologiques sur la corde du tympan, pour servir à l'histoire de l'hémiplégie faciale,"[1] followed, in December of the same year by his "Thèse pour le Doctorat en médecine" having for title "Du suc gastrique et de son rôle dans la nutrition."

The work on the chorda tympani, in which we may recognise the influence of Magendie's long continued labours on the functions of nerves, is in part anatomical and in part physiological. The former part is one of the many illustrations of Bernard's exact and extensive anatomical knowledge, in acquiring which he was greatly aided by

[1] "Annales médico-psychologiques," I., 1843, p. 408.

EARLY LABOURS

his remarkable manual dexterity in dissection, a knowledge and dexterity which some years later was displayed in his contributions to Huette's popular work on surgical anatomy. In the physiological part he deals chiefly with the relations of the nerve to taste and hearing ; and it is interesting to note that though he was destined hereafter to carry out many important researches, of which the action of the chorda tympani on the submaxillary gland was the pivot, so that this first memoir serves in a certain sense as the beginning of long series of investigations on the relations of nerves to secretion, he began by a false step. He contended that the chorda had no influence on the secretory activity of the submaxillary gland or on the contractile efforts of its duct.

The thesis on the gastric juice was still more emphatically the first of a long series

CLAUDE BERNARD

of investigations; as we shall see it was the first step in an inquiry which before long led him to the discovery of the glycogenic function of the liver. The main result made known in the thesis was that while cane sugar injected directly into the veins readily appeared in the urine, this did not occur when the cane sugar, previous to the injection, had been subjected to the influence of the gastric juice. He inferred that cane sugar as such in the blood was unsuitable for the nutrition of the tissues, and was consequently cast out, but that by the influence of gastric juice it was so modified as to become suitable, and in that condition was retained and utilised. In this simple result lay the germ of much that was to come afterwards. The paper is also interesting as containing the record of the experiment which has since become classical, of the simultaneous injection of potassium ferro-

EARLY LABOURS

cyanide, and ferrous sulphate, by which he showed that the acid of gastric juice makes its appearance on the surface and not in the depths of the gastric glands.

These two researches in a way illustrate, when put together, the main idea which governed almost the entire course of Bernard's labours. The action of the nervous system on the chemical changes which constitute the basis of nutrition, was a problem always present to his mind, and one which he attempted to solve on the one hand by experimental investigations on nerves, and on the other by direct chemical researches; he was almost always busy with the one or with the other, and happy when he was employing the two methods at the same time and in concert.

The reference to facial paralysis in his paper on the chorda, indicates also that from the outset of his career he had grasped the view that physiology may fitly be called experimental medicine, the results of the laboratory being, with due precautions, available for use at the bedside.

His succeeding researches were carried out much on the same line as the first two. He investigated the spinal accessory nerve, and he continued his studies in digestion, and other problems of chemical physiology, sending in for his thesis at the "Concours pour l'agrégation" a memoir on the colouring matters present in the human body.

No very remarkable result was obtained in any of the above researches, but in the year 1846, in the course of an investigation on the differences in digestion and nutrition between herbivora and carnivora, an investigation which he carried on, as he did many of his earlier chemical researches, in company with his friend Barreswil, he made an observation which proved to be the

EARLY LABOURS

starting-point of his first really important discovery.

"We had observed," says he,[1] "that when we introduced fat into the stomach of a rabbit, the fat passing on from the stomach was not modified until it had reached a certain distance from the stomach at a point much lower than that at which a like change takes place in the case of dogs. The same difference manifested itself in the absorption of the fat by the lacteals. We saw that these in the rabbit first became white and opaque through the presence of fat at a considerable distance from the pylorus, whereas in dogs the change was visible at the very commencement of the duodenum. This difference between dogs and rabbits as to the place at which the modification and

[1] Leçons de Physiologie Expérimentale. Cours. 1855, II., p. 178.

absorption of fat begins to take place having been confirmed by repeated observation, it was natural to look for the cause in some special disposition of the intestines; and now we noted that the difference coincided with a difference in the entrance of the pancreatic duct into the intestine. In the dog the pancreatic juice is discharged into the intestine quite close to the pylorus, whereas in the rabbit the principal pancreatic duct opens into the intestine at a point thirty or thirty-five centimetres below the opening of the biliary duct. It was precisely at this point that the change in the fat began to take place, and that the lacteals were able to absorb it."

This observation was the starting-point of Bernard's remarkable researches on the properties and uses of the pancreas. And it may be noted that in this, as indeed

EARLY LABOURS

in some other instances, Bernard was led to an important truth by an observation not wholly accurate. It was pointed out afterwards, and has become generally accepted, that this disposition of the fat and the lacteal contents in the rabbit is not invariable, indeed, that the appearances described by Bernard are seen not always, but only when the abdomen is opened at a particular time after the taking of the fat. Nevertheless, the observation did start Bernard on a fruitful inquiry into the action of the pancreatic juice, and with that instinct of genius which was one of his marked characteristics, he deserted the search into the differences between herbivora and carnivora for the new line of investigation which the observation in question suggested.

The new research was not, however, completed for some little time. The first

CLAUDE BERNARD

notice of the results obtained were made known to the Société Philomathique in April, 1848, and a somewhat fuller account was presented to the Société de Biologie in February, 1849. Yet it was not until 1856 that he published the complete " Mémoire sur le pancreas et sur le rôle du suc pancréatique," which appeared as a supplement to the "Comptes Rendus" of the Académie des Sciences for that year.

At the time when Bernard took the matter in hand our knowledge of the action of the pancreatic juice, and indeed of intestinal digestion was of the scantiest. In Johannes Müller's great work, pages are devoted to gastric digestion, Beaumont's observations on Alexis St. Martin, the Canadian with the accidental gastric fistula, being dwelt upon at length ; indeed, the changes undergone by the food in the stomach are treated as if they were almost

EARLY LABOURS

identical with digestion as a whole. A good deal is said it is true about the bile; but the pancreas is passed over almost in silence. " The excellent researches of Tiedemann and Gmelin" are quoted as containing "all that we know with certainty relative to the changes which the chyme undergoes in the intestine;" and all that these authors have to suggest is the possibility "that the casein of the pancreatic secretion containing a large proportion of nitrogen yields a portion of this element to different ingredients of the alimentary substances which contain less nitrogen, so as to reduce itself to their standard in this respect, and to convert them into albumen."

Let this vague conception be compared with the knowledge which we at present have of the several distinct actions of the pancreatic juice, and of the predominant importance of this fluid not only in intestinal digestion, but in digestion as a whole, and it will be at once seen what a great advance has taken place in this matter since the early forties. That advance we owe in the main to Bernard. Valentin, it is true, had in 1844 not only inferred that the pancreatic juice had an action on starch, but confirmed his view by actual experiment with the juice expressed from the gland; and Eberle had suggested that the juice had some action on fat; but Bernard at one stroke made clear its threefold action. He showed that it, on the one hand, emulsified, and, on the other hand, split up into fatty acids and glycerine, the neutral fats discharged from the stomach into the duodenum; he clearly proved that it had a powerful action on starch, converting it into sugar; and, lastly, he laid bare its remarkable action on proteid matters.

EARLY LABOURS

Pointing out that the bile precipitates the products of the gastric digestion of proteid matters, and puts an end to peptic changes, he went on to show that the pancreatic juice acted subsequently as well on these precipitated matters as on those proteid constituents of a meal which had escaped solution in the stomach. "It is, in fact, the pancreatic juice which has the special property of completely dissolving these two kinds of material, for the digestion of nitrogenous substances is far from being completed in the stomach, though this is the accepted view. Two acts, perfectly distinct, take place in the stomach, and in the intestine, the one duly following the other. Gastric digestion is only a preparatory act." In carrying out the observations which supply the proof of this energetic and multiple action of the pancreatic juice, Bernard took a hint from Blondlot, who in

CLAUDE BERNARD

1843 had introduced the method of the artificial gastric fistula. He not only himself early and repeatedly used the gastric fistula, but, extending the method, brought into use the pancreatic fistula. Regnier de Graaf had, it is true, so early as 1662, succeeded in making some sort of pancreatic fistula, but in a very imperfect and fruitless manner. It was Bernard who made the operation really practicable and useful.

When we realise how deeply our present knowledge of the varied and powerful action of pancreatic juice has affected our present conceptions, not only of the digestive act, but also of the processes of nutrition, and when we remember that, making all allowance for the researches, subsequent to those of Bernard, of Corvisait, and especially of Kühne, on the proteolytic action of the juice, not only the

EARLY LABOURS

foundation, but even the larger part of the whole edifice of that knowledge, is to be found in Bernard's memoir, we may be well prepared to commend the action of the Académie des Sciences, when in 1850 it awarded to the researches embodied in that memoir the prize of Experimental Physiology.

By the publication of that memoir, moreover, not only France, but men of science in all lands, were made aware that a young physiological inquirer of striking powers had arisen in Paris. Yet the merits of the research on the pancreas were soon to be eclipsed by results of a still higher order, and of far more commanding influence, reached by the efforts of the same brilliant investigator.

Before we leave these earlier labours, however, one more research must be mentioned, a research in which Bernard came to the aid of his master, Magendie. In supplying in 1822 the direct and complete proof of C. Bell's views as to the separate functions of the anterior and posterior roots of spinal nerves, and in later experiments of the same kind in 1829 and 1839, Magendie had sometimes found the anterior roots sensitive. He, however (or Longet, for this observer claimed the merit of the observation), also observed that this sensibility of the anterior root was in some way dependent on the posterior root, was a sensibility imparted to the anterior root and not inherent, like the sensibility of the posterior root in the root itself; and the sensibility in question accordingly received the name of " recurrent sensibility." The phenomena, however, were exceedingly inconstant; sometimes the anterior root was found to be sensitive, but more often the

EARLY LABOURS

results of a search for sensibility were negative. So uncertain was the matter that Longet was ultimately led to deny altogether the existence of any such thing as recurrent sensibility.

Bernard, attending Magendie's course in 1839, and witnessing the inconstant results of the experiments on this recurrent sensibility, concluded, with the quick insight of a true inquirer, that the inconstancy must be due to a want of knowledge of the conditions under which the experiment ought to be conducted. And he set about to determine what those conditions were. A few years later he had laid hold of the conditions, and in 1847 he published two papers [1] in which, by showing what circumstances favoured and what hindered the development of

[1] "Soc. Philom.," 1847, p. 79, and "Comptes Rendus," xxv. pp. 104, 106, 1847.

recurrent sensibility, he rescued his master's discovery from the disrepute into which it had fallen. The experiments and arguments briefly summarised in the two papers just spoken of are more fully set forth in the lectures on the nervous system which Bernard published many years later. The question of recurrent sensibility does not possess to-day the importance which it seemed to have then; the researches of Bernard in relation to it are worthy however of special note, since they bear the marks of the same power to solve an experimental problem, which later on brought in such rich results.

> Bernard's published lectures on Nerves

IV

GLYCOGEN

IMPORTANT as was Bernard's discovery of the action of the pancreatic juice, he soon came upon a far greater one. And the story of how he came upon it is worth telling in detail, since it illustrates in a striking manner how an alert, inquiring mind, seizing at once upon the hints which Nature gave, was led into a wholly new path, and, cautiously advancing step by step, as the way opened up, was enabled, by almost its own unassisted labours, to give to the world a new truth,

CLAUDE BERNARD

not as a mere rough conception, but as a highly finished work.

At the time when Bernard began his physiological studies, the views which the great Dumas had brilliantly expounded in the "Essai sur la Statique Chimique des Êtres Organisés," written by himself and the agronomic chemist Boussingault, may be said to have been dominant among biologists. According to those views, animals and plants presented a complete chemical contrast, the one to the other. The chemical token of the plant was that out of the elements existing in the inorganic world it built up the complex organic compounds, the carbohydrates, the fats, the proteids, and the like, which formed the chemical basis of its body. The chemical token of the animal was that, by feeding, it received these ready-made organic compounds into its body,

GLYCOGEN

and destroyed them, resolving them again into inorganic constituents, and utilising that resolution for the needs of its life. The animal might modify the vegetable compounds and give them an animal character; but it never made anything anew. Matter passed through a cycle rising up through the constructive labours of the plant into the organic compounds of the living body, and falling back again by the destructive labours of the animal into the inorganic compounds of the world which was not alive. The contrast was held to be complete; it was asserted that the animal body never built up, never manufactured, either fat, or carbohydrate, or proteid; all of any of these present in the animal body had been brought to it in its food.

These were the dominant views, though the voice of heresy had already made itself

CLAUDE BERNARD

heard. In the spring of 1843, the year in which Bernard published his first papers, the calm of the Académie des Sciences was broken by a lively discussion. Payen, a chemist who was an authority on the chemistry of food, communicated a paper by Dumas, Boussingault, and himself,[1] in which it was insisted that the fat already present in the fodder was, as shown by careful analysis, sufficient to supply the fat found in the body of the fattened beast. Liebig intervened in the discussion by a letter in which he quoted new experiments by Gundlach at Giessen, confirming Huber's old observations of 1780, that bees fed on sugar alone formed wax, and disproving the criticism that the bees had furnished the wax out of the previous store of fat in their own bodies. He further showed that

[1] " Recherches sur l'engraissement des bestiaux et la formation du lait."

GLYCOGEN

the fat accumulated in the bodies of fattened geese far exceeded the supply furnished by the fat of their food, and while twitting Dumas for refusing to believe that starch or sugar could be changed into fat, while he assumed that mere waxy material could be so changed, though the change was, from a chemical laboratory point of view, almost as difficult, clenched his argument by showing that when a cow was fattened, the excreta during the fattening period contained as much fat as the food taken. Dumas and his friends remained apparently unconvinced, though, by an irony of fate, in the very next year Dumas announced to the Academy that observations conducted by Milne-Edwards and himself on bees fully confirmed the validity of Huber's old argument.

It was while men's opinions on the chemistry of nutrition were in this con-

CLAUDE BERNARD

dition that Bernard took up a research on the physiology of sugar. His second published paper, his thesis for the doctorate, on the action of the gastric juice, was the initial step in this research. His active mind, in turning from poetry to science, had lost nothing of its early ambition. The task which he had proposed to himself was no less a one than to trace out the successive transformations which the food stuffs, the dominant substances of food, underwent within the animal body. His first result, embodied in his thesis, was that cane sugar was acted upon by gastric juice, and underwent through the influence of that fluid its first transformation, namely, a change into dextrose (glucose) as a necessary preparation for its being utilised by the tissues.

He had intended to study all the three great classes of food stuffs, carbohydrates,

GLYCOGEN

fats and proteids ; but he began with the first, and found the study of these so expansive that he never got beyond them. He began with sugars, partly because they were the more simple, and partly because he had become early fascinated with the problems suggested by the disease diabetes; he was anxious to explain the cause of this excess of sugar in diabetes, and so by good fortune to find a remedy for it.

The plan of research which he marked out for himself was somewhat as follows. Tiedemann and Gmelin had shown that in the alimentary canal starch is converted into dextrose before being absorbed ; he had himself shown, as we have just said, that cane-sugar—sugar of the first species, as he called it—is also converted into dextrose, into sugar of the second species. All carbohydrates, then, may be considered as passing into the blood as dextrose.

CLAUDE BERNARD

What becomes of this dextrose? What fate, what transformation, awaits it? Bernard proposed to himself to track out diligently the dextrose, introduced into the body from the alimentary canal, along the portal vein to the liver, from the liver through the right heart to the lungs, and then from the lungs through the left heart to the several tissues of the body. "At one or other of these stations I shall find," he said to himself, "that the dextrose disappears, is destroyed, or is in some way or other changed. If, having found the station of destruction, I am able to suppress the activity of this station, sugar will accumulate in the blood, and a condition of diabetes will be brought about. (He had already satisfied himself that the essence of diabetes was an excess of sugar in the blood.) If I can thus artificially produce diabetes, the way will be opened for the

GLYCOGEN

discovery of curative means." All this he tells us himself[1]; the great discovery he was about to make was no haphazard dive in Nature's full pocket; it was the reward of a carefully planned enterprise. And the crown fell into his hands in this wise.

He fed a dog on a diet rich in sugar and sugar-furnishing material, and, killing it at the height of digestion, examined the blood leaving the liver by the hepatic veins, to to see if there were any destruction of sugar in the liver. It is perhaps worthy of notice as illustrating how "there is a time for everything," how many things, some of them little, contribute to a result, that the search for sugar in the tissues and fluids of the animal body, to which Bernard had set himself, was just at that time rendered much easier by Bernard's friend

[1] "Nouvelle fonction du foie."

and fellow worker, the chemist Barreswil, having introduced the cupric sulphate test for dextrose, the test which in a slightly modified form we now use a Fehling's test. Bernard found abundant sugar in the blood of the hepatic veins. The liver, therefore, was not the sought for seat of the disappearance of dextrose. "But," said Bernard to himself, "how do I know that the sugar which I thus find in the hepatic vein, is the same sugar as that which I introduced into the portal blood through the food?" He accordingly fed another dog on meat only, on sheep's head, having previously satisfied himself that, under these circumstances no dextrose was present either in the alimentary canal or the portal blood, and again examined the blood of the hepatic vein.

To his great astonishment he found that

GLYCOGEN

in this case also the blood of the hepatic vein was loaded with dextrose.

Here came in the genius of the true inquirer. "Why!" said he, "if I have made no mistakes, I have in this experiment come upon the production of sugar: the liver produces sugar. I need not labour at the long task which I had marked out for myself, of searching for the seat of the destruction, the disappearance of sugar, so that by suppressing that I might indirectly bring about the accumulation of sugar. If the result which I have just got is confirmed on repetition of the experiment, the liver is a sugar-producing tissue, it manufactures sugar out of something which is not sugar, and within it lies the secret of diabetes. Further, Dumas is wrong in saying that animals do not construct, that the liver does not construct; the liver does construct, it constructs dextrose. This is a big thing of which I have got hold. I must make sure that there is no mistake in the experiment, and then push forward as far as possible the lead thus given me."

He set about to test his result in every possible way. He took dogs which had been starved, and dogs which had been fed for some time on meat alone, and found in both cases that sugar, while absent from the alimentary canal and from the chyle, was present in the blood of the right heart and in the blood of the portal vein close to the liver. He starved a dog for several days in order to get rid of the effects of a previous mixed diet, then fed it on meat, and found sugar as before in the hepatic vein and right heart. Opening the body of a dog killed in full digestion he placed ligatures on the mesenteric veins at some little distance from the intestine, on the

GLYCOGEN

veins from the pancreas, on the splenic vein, and on the vena portæ near the liver; he found no sugar in the blood of the mesenteric veins between the intestine and the ligature, none in the blood of the pancreatic or splenic veins, but there was sugar in the portal blood between the ligature and the liver. Obviously, the sugar in the latter case had regurgitated from the liver; it was clear that the liver, and not the spleen or the pancreas, any more than the food in the intestine, was the source of the sugar. And he found that a simple decoction of the liver substance invariably contained sugar. Lastly, he determined that the sugar in question was dextrose, was a sugar capable of fermentation, and giving all the ordinary tests for dextrose.

He now felt justified in making known to the world that the liver was capable of

CLAUDE BERNARD

producing sugar not brought to it as sugar in the food, that sugar made its appearance in the liver itself by an act which seemed very analogous to the act of secretion by a secreting gland, and which therefore might be spoken of as an internal secretion. On the 28th of August, he deposited a sealed packet with the Académie des Sciences, and on the 15th of November following, he and Barreswil exhibited at the Académie a specimen of alcohol obtained by fermentation from sugar of the liver, their efforts to crystallise the sugar having so far been unsuccessful. In 1849 he laid before the Société de Biologie a fuller account of his researches,[1] and again in 1850 before the Académie des Sciences.[2]

Continuing his researches, examining the

[1] "Mém. Soc. Biol.," 1849, pp. 121–133.
[2] "Compt. Rend.," xxi. p. 571 ; 1850, pp. 571–574.

GLYCOGEN

livers of many different kinds of vertebrate animals, and indeed of invertebrate animals also, he found full confirmation of his view that the sugar of the liver is not supplied directly from the food, but is furnished by the liver itself, through a mechanism analogous to that of secretion, at the expense of elements of the blood which traverse the hepatic tissue. He early recognised, however, that this hepatic sugar, though it did not come direct from the food, was influenced as regards its quantity by the nature of the food. Thus he observed that it was much diminished, even to disappearance, by long starvation, that it was very little if at all increased by fatty food, but was very markedly increased by gelatine or by carbohydrates. This influence of food and other influences such as that of age, as well as the action of the nervous system, he more fully expounded in the thesis which he maintained for his Doctorate in Science, on March 17, 1853, and which was published as a monograph in the same year.

In the course of these researches he had come upon the remarkable fact that puncture of the fourth ventricle causes temporary diabetes. The first record of this is a note communicated to the Société de Biologie,[1] in which the author stated that he had previously shown the same effect in rabbits; no published account, however, of this appears. The same fact was also announced in a brief note to the Académie des Sciences.[2]

It is interesting to note the way in which Bernard was led to this striking result.

---

[1] "Compt. Rend. Soc. Biol.," 1849, p. 60 (April), "Chiens rendus diabétiques."
[2] "Compt. Rend.," xxviii. p. 393.

GLYCOGEN

At first sight it has the appearance of being an accidental result; and the fact that so early as February 3, 1849,[1] Bernard had stated that section of the cerebellar peduncles led to the appearance of albumin and sugar in the urine, lends a certain amount of support to this idea. But, according to Bernard himself, he was led to it by a process of reasoning.

Regarding, as he had come to do, the appearance of the sugar as a secretion—an internal secretion of the liver—he argued that this secretion, like other secretions, would be subject to the influence of an appropriate nerve. Anatomical considerations, as well as earlier observations on the vagus, and its relations to digestion,[2] led him to suppose that the nerve in question could be none

[1] "Compt. Rend. de la Soc. Biol.," 1849, p. 14.
[2] "Compt. Rend.," xviii., 1844, p. 995, &c.

CLAUDE BERNARD

other than the vagus nerve. And he was confirmed in this view by the fact which he had early ascertained that section of the vagus nerves did away with the formation of the sugar. He accordingly expected to find that galvanic stimulation of the vagus trunks would lead to an increase of the hepatic sugar; but in this he was grievously disappointed; all his results were negative. Remembering, however, some older experiments of his on the fifth pair, in which he had produced secretory effects—tears and saliva—by irritating the nerve in a special way, namely, by puncturing it at its origin in the brain, he conceived the idea of applying the same method to the vagus at its origin in the floor of the fourth ventricle. The experiment succeeded, the sugar-producing or glycogenic function of the liver was thereby highly excited; so much sugar

GLYCOGEN

was poured so rapidly into the blood stream that it could not be disposed of, and, like an excess of sugar in the blood produced by artificial injection, made its way into the urine. Bernard himself was one of the first to recognise that the theoretical view which led him to this remarkable result was founded on error, that the vagus is not the channel by which the influences, started by the puncture of the fourth ventricle, whatever be their nature, reach and affect the liver, that the vagus is not the secretory nerve governing the secretion of hepatic sugar. Nevertheless the wrong view led him to an important truth ; and indeed it was one of Bernard's characteristics that his experimental search after new facts was never a haphazard prodding into unknown ground ; he was always guided by some preconceived theory, sometimes right but more often perhaps wrong. No less a characteristic, and this was perhaps the one which led him so far, was his readiness to fasten on to the new fact, and to consider it by itself, regardless of the theory which had led him to it. In all his writings he insists on the value of imagination and preconceived theory in experimental research; but he knew how to use them and when to throw them on one side. He used to say to those who were working with them, "Put off your imagination as you take off your overcoat when you enter the laboratory; but put it on again, as you do the overcoat, when you leave the laboratory. Before the experiment and between whiles let your imagination wrap you round; put it right away from yourself during the experiment itself, lest it hinder your observing power."

GLYCOGEN

By these continued observations, confirmed as they speedily were by investigators elsewhere, notably by Lehmann in Leipzig, though criticised and controverted as they were by others, more especially perhaps in France itself, Bernard had established the glycogenic function of the liver; he had proved that the liver produces sugar by means of a mechanism analogous to that of secretion at the expense of the elements of the blood traversing the hepatic tissue.

But he did not stop here.

He soon came to the conclusion that the sugar was not formed at one step out of the elements, whatever they might be, which the blood brought to the liver, but that the sugar came from some substance existing in the hepatic tissue, some substance capable of being converted into sugar, some "glycogenic substance." He was led to this conclusion in the following way.

Taking a liver fresh from the body, he sent a stream of water through it until the wash-water issuing by the hepatic vein contained neither albumin nor sugar. He washed out of the liver all the sugar previously present in it, and a decoction of the liver so washed out contained no sugar. But if the liver thus washed out and sugarless were allowed to remain, especially in a warm place, for some time, say for a few hours, a subsequent stream sent through the vessels was once more loaded with sugar, as was also a decoction of the liver substance. The sugar had been washed out by the first washing, but not the glycogenic substance, and this latter had subsequently given rise to fresh sugar.

He next found that the conversion of

this glycogenic substance into actual sugar was arrested by the hepatic tissue being subjected to the temperature of boiling water. Aware of the profound changes which proteid matter undergoes when subjected to the above temperature, his first idea was that his "glycogenic substance" was of a proteid nature, and that its conversion into sugar was prevented by the changes of composition induced in it by the high temperature. But he was soon set right by the observation that a decoction of boiled liver, though of itself it remained unchanged, producing no sugar, readily gave rise to sugar when a small quantity of an infusion of fresh, unboiled liver was added to it. He saw at once that the conversion of his glycogenic substance was brought about by a kind of fermentation, that the glycogenic substance itself was of the nature of starch. By straining the liver decoction free from blood-vessels and connective tissue elements, he was, by subsequent washing with alcohol and ether, able to prepare, in the form of a dry powder, a glycogenic substance, which, not itself giving the tests for dextrose, was readily converted by fermentation into dextrose. These important results he communicated to the Académie des Sciences on Sept. 24, 1855.[1]

His powdered liver, however, was still a very impure substance, and it was not until March 23, 1857,[2] that he could describe the complete isolation by the now well-known potash-alcohol process, and the definite characters of the substance which he now felt justified in

[1] "Compt. Rend.," xli. p. 461, "Sur le méchanisme de la formation du sucre dans le foie."

[2] "Compt. Rend.," xliv. p. 578, "Sur le méchanisme," &c., (suite).

GLYCOGEN

calling *glycogen*. He obtained this in a sufficiently pure form to enable Pelouze, as the result of an elementary analysis, to assert its carbohydrate nature. He had, earlier in the year,[1] given some account of these results to the Société de Biologie; and it may here be mentioned that Hensen[2] had independently been led to accomplish the isolation of glycogen.

In the above memoir Bernard describes the technique for the extraction and purification of glycogen, and gives an account of its reactions, including that towards iodine. He adds some valuable reflections on the whole subject, pointing out that while the formation of glycogen is a vital act, that is to say, takes place only under conditions of life, the conversion of glycogen into dextrose, by a process of

[1] "Mém. Soc. Biol.," 1857, pp. 1–7.
[2] "Verhl. d. Phys. Med. Gesell. Würzburg," Bd. viii., 1856, s. 219.

fermentation, is independent of life. He calls attention to the fact that the blood contains in itself a ferment capable of converting glycogen into dextrose, and suggests that the nervous system, in giving rise to an increase of sugar, as in the diabetic puncture, probably acts in an indirect manner by modifying in some way the circulation. He further draws an interesting comparison between glycogen and sugar in the liver, and starch and sugar in a germinating seed; in the one glycogen, in the other starch, is formed and deposited in the cell by virtue of the living activities of the tissue, in both the carbohydrate so formed is converted into sugar by the action of a ferment.

This brings to a close the first chapter of the history of glycogen. It was Bernard's good fortune not only to have

GLYCOGEN

begun but to have completed the discovery. Though the whole investigation took several years to accomplish, though from the very outset the matter excited great interest throughout the whole scientific world, and many other hands were put to the work, it was Bernard himself who, following steadfastly the lead given by his initial observation, through successive steps, each new one reached by trials based on sound reasoning suggested by its forerunner, arrived at the final goal. Though he never shrank from making known each new result as he came upon it, he had not the mortification, which sometimes falls to a pioneer, of seeing his leading conceptions realised by experimental proof in the hands of others before he himself has had time to furnish the decisive evidence. The whole story lies in Bernard's own writings. To the account which he gives of his own researches, the rest of contemporary literature on the subject, whether we consider the corroborative writings of Lehmann and others, or the opposing views offered by Figuier, Sanson, and others, appears as a mere unimportant fringe. Nor can much importance be attached to the mere fact that Hensen was prior to Bernard in publishing an account of the isolation of glycogen, since Bernard had practically effected the isolation some time before. Bernard started the fox, was at the head of the pack through the whole run, and was first in at the death.

Every discovery in physiology of any marked magnitude has a double bearing. On the one hand, it is a link in a chain, or rather a network, of special problems; it serves as a starting-point of new inquiries, and fills up gaps in, or it may be supplies corrections to, old ones. On the other hand,

GLYCOGEN

it influences more or less deeply, according to its nature, general physiological conceptions. Bernard's discovery of the glycogenic function of the liver was powerful in both these directions. As a mere contribution to the history of sugar within the animal body, as a link in the chain of special problems connected with digestion and nutrition, its value was very great. Even greater, perhaps, was its effect as a contribution to general views.

The view that the animal body, in contrast to the plant, could not construct, could only destroy, was, as we have seen, already being shaken. But evidence, however strong, offered in the form of statistical calculations, of numerical comparisons between income and output, failed to produce anything like the conviction which was brought home to every one by the demonstration that a substance was actually formed within the animal body and by the exhibition of the substance so formed.

No less revolutionary was the demonstration that the liver had other things to do in the animal economy besides secreting bile. This, at one blow, destroyed the then dominant conception that the animal body was to be regarded as a bundle of organs, each with its appropriate function, a conception which did much to narrow inquiry, since when a suitable function had once been assigned to an organ there seemed no need for further investigation. Physiology, expounded as it often was at that time, in the light of such a conception, was apt to leave in the mind of the hearer the view that what remained to be done consisted chiefly in determining the use of organs such as the spleen, to which as yet no definite function had been allotted. The discovery of the glycogenic function of the

GLYCOGEN

liver struck a heavy blow at the whole theory of functions.

No less pregnant of future discoveries was the idea suggested by this newly found out action of the hepatic tissue, the idea happily formulated by Bernard as "internal secretion." No part of physiology is at the present day being more fruitfully studied than that which deals with the changes which the blood undergoes as it sweeps through the several tissues, changes by the careful adaptation of which what we call the health of the body is secured, changes the failure or discordance of which entails disease. The study of these internal secretions constitutes a path of inquiry which has already been trod with conspicuous success, and which promises to lead to untold discoveries of the greatest moment; the gate to this path was opened by Bernard's work.

CLAUDE BERNARD

With the demonstration of the actual substance the first chapter of the story of glycogen is, as we have said, closed. By it the mode of inquiry was profoundly changed and a new chapter begun. The search for indications of the appearance of sugar was replaced for a search for the substance glycogen. And Bernard himself was the first to contribute to the new chapter. He had quite early in his investigation come across and appreciated the importance of the fact that sugar is formed in the liver of the embryo after a certain stage of intra-uterine life and that sugar is present in the anmiotic and allantoic fluids. He was now armed with two new methods of inquiry. In the first place, he could quantitatively determine the amount of glycogen present in this or that tissue under these or those circumstances ; this gave a precision to his results which could never be gained by a mere estimation of the production of sugar. In the second place, he early recognised that the colour reaction of glycogen towards iodine, the port-wine colour which glycogen showed when treated with iodine under favourable circumstances, enabled him to study the ways of glycogen not only by chemical but also by histological investigation, the one method of investigation confirming or checking the other.

In purely histological inquiries Bernard was not " at home " ; but in the microscopical search after glycogen he was able to avail himself of the skilful help of a young German then studying under him, one who was already becoming known by a remarkable research in the physiology of muscle, and who has since achieved a foremost place among the physiologists of the day, Willie Kühne,· the distinguished professor of Heidelberg. In saying that

CLAUDE BERNARD

Bernard did not seem to have the same facility in histological as in other physiological inquiries, this must be understood to apply to the technique only. In grasping the meaning of histological facts, he showed the same quick power which characterised him in all his work. He, for instance, early recognised the significance of the granules in the secreting cells of the pancreas; and indeed Kühne, to whom, after Bernard, so much of our knowledge of the pancreas is due, gave to these granules the name of " Bernard's granules."

The fruits of the new method he made known to the Académie des Sciences in 1859.[1] In a series of papers he gave an account of the presence of glycogen on the one hand in the maternal placenta, and, on the other hand, in various

[1] "Compt. Rend.," xlviii. pp. 77, 673, 884.

GLYCOGEN

fœtal tissues, calling attention especially to the relatively enormous quantity of glycogen present in developing striated muscles. With characteristic breadth of view he dwells on the light which the presence of this carbohydrate in tissues while they are struggling to put on their appropriate structure, throws on the nature of the processes of nutrition.

This may, perhaps, be considered as Bernard's last important contribution to the history of glycogen. He, it is true, continued to work on the subject to the end of his life. In his last year, in 1877, he contributed three papers upon it to the Académie des Sciences, having in the interval between that and 1859 published other papers, and more especially made known the results of fresh experiments, and developed general views in his lectures delivered at the Collége de

CLAUDE BERNARD

France and elsewhere. The volume of lectures on Diabetes ("Leçons sur le Diabète") published in 1877 may be considered as his last testament touching the subject.

All these later writings, however, are chiefly occupied in expounding or defending his views on the nature and purpose of the glycogenic function, or in criticising the opinions on the same subject expressed by others.

Not a little space in them is from time to time devoted to a severe criticism on what he called the vitalistic view put forward by some, and more especially by his pupil Pavy, teaching that the appearance of sugar in the liver is a *post-mortem* phenomena. Bernard, as we have seen, had taken up a definite position in relation to questions of so-called " vitalism " ; and if ever he was tempted to abandon the tone

GLYCOGEN

of calm and dispassionate attitude in which he discussed most questions, it was when he had to deal with vitalistic theories. His very last paper but one, that in the " Comptes Rendus " of 1877, deals trenchantly with this view of the *post-mortem* character of the appearance of hepatic sugar; and in his lectures on Diabetes he cannot resist the temptation to be sarcastic when discussing it, pointing out that according to it " a diabetic patient is a walking corpse ; a truly droll idea."

The reader who reads these various later writings in the light of the knowledge which we possess to-day cannot but be struck with the reflection that if we put aside the discovery of share taken by the pancreas in determining the part played by sugar in the animal body, all that has since been added by others to Bernard's own results, amounts, compared with them,

CLAUDE BERNARD

to something relatively small. It has rarely fallen to the lot of any one, who made the beginning of such a wholly new line of research, to carry it forward so far towards completion with his own hands as Bernard did the glycogenic function of the liver. The views which he left behind him in 1877 have, on the whole, not been largely modified by subsequent inquiry. Much, for instance, has been done since that in determining the influence of carbohydrate food on the storage of hepatic glycogen; but it is worthy of notice that Bernard early recognised this, and that in spite of the fact that the corner-stone of his whole discovery consisted in the proof that sugar in the hepatic vein was independent of sugar in the alimentary canal.

So also in many other details the kernel of what we are discussing to-day may be found in some sentence or other of

GLYCOGEN

Bernard's. It has been the fate of many other men in many matters to have merely laid a foundation on which other men have built. He, in the matter of glycogen, not only laid the very first stone, but left a house so nearly finished that other men have been able to add but little.

V

VASO-MOTOR NERVES

THE discovery of glycogen was Bernard's greatest achievement; next in importance to this, and, indeed, hardly less than it, was his discovery of the vaso-motor system. The part which he played in this latter discovery, however, was very different from that which he played in the former. As we have just said, he not only began but carried out and, we may almost say, completed the discovery of glycogen by his own researches; the contributions of others in his own time were almost insignificant as compared with

VASO-MOTOR NERVES

his. He, moreover, at the very outset grasped the full and almost the exact meaning of what he had laid hold of.

In the case of the vaso-motor nerves, it was others rather than himself who first recognised the importance of his earlier result, the vaso-motor function of the cervical sympathetic. In the case of this, as in the case of glycogen, he was looking for something else when he found it. But, unlike his attitude in the glycogenic research, he did not at once turn aside and give himself up to the new result. It would almost seem as if he did not at first see its importance, and was inclined to continue on the line of inquiry which he had originally laid out for himself; and, indeed, to this he clung to the end, though the interest which others manifested in the intercurrent vaso-motor phenomena led him, in spite almost of himself, to develop this part of the inquiry.

Before proceeding to speak of Bernard's investigation, it will be well perhaps to call to mind what was the condition of our knowledge at that time of the relation of the nervous system to the blood-vessels.

The great German physiologist, Johannes Müller, in the 1838 edition of his classical work on Physiology, the English translation of which by Baily appeared in 1841 and 1843, recognises two kinds of muscle, the striated muscles, the muscles of the trunk and limbs, and the non-striated muscles of organic life found in the intestines, the uterus, the bladder, and the iris. He also describes the contractile "cellular" or "connective" tissue, as we now call it ; of this the dartos of the scrotum serves as his characteristic example. He distinguishes this from muscle by the fact

VASO-MOTOR NERVES

of its yielding gelatine, whereas muscles, he says, are fibrinous. He discusses at great length the question whether arteries possess muscular contractility, and decides firmly in the negative; they possess physical elasticity, but not muscular contractility. He admits, however, the possibility that the contraction observed in small vessels upon the application of cold, as insisted upon more especially by Schwann, may be a manifestation of that which he, in the language initiated by Bichat, speaks of as "insensible organic contractility," and which was supposed to be the basis of the "tonus" not only of the tissues of organic life, but even of the skeletal muscles. Müller obviously was wholly unprepared for vaso-motor nerves, even within a few years of Bernard's discovery of them.

The fact, however, that the sympathetic nerves were in many places traced to blood-

CLAUDE BERNARD

vessels was leading men to suspect that the nervous system must in some way govern the blood-vessels. In 1840 Henle, discoursing on the physiology of "sympathy," and putting to himself the question why do sympathetic fibres, apparently motor in nature, go to such structures as arteries if these, as supposed, are devoid of muscles, was led to the conclusion that the middle coat of the arteries is really in part muscular in nature, though the muscular tissue in them is of a kind somewhat different from that, not only of the skeletal muscles, but also of such muscles as those of the intestine. And in the same year Stilling, in a work on "Spinal Irritation," had introduced the word "vasomotor." Arguing on theoretical grounds he had come to the conclusion that there were motor nerves not subject to the will but capable of being put into action by

VASO-MOTOR NERVES

sensory impulses, nerves which determined the movements of the blood, and which he therefore proposed to call "vaso-motor nerves."

A little later on the whole question of the muscular nature of the blood-vessels and other allied tissues was made clear through the discovery by Kölliker in 1846 of the fact that plain muscular tissue, whether occurring in masses or in a scattered fashion, was made up of minute spindle shaped cells aggregated together.

The way was now open for the clear proof of the existence and action of vaso-motor nerves; but no one supplied this until Bernard came upon it. And his discovery was made in this way.

He proposed for himself the study of the influence of the nervous system on animal heat; and he began by attempting to ascertain in an exact manner how far the temperature of a part of the body was affected by the section of the nerve or nerves distributed to it. Of the three kinds of nerves, at that time distinguished from each other, motor, sensory, and sympathetic, he began with the sympathetic, being led to this choice by the consideration that the sympathetic fibres, since they so often accompany the blood-vessels, are probably specially connected with the chemical changes between the blood and the tissue which determine the development of heat and so the temperature of the part.

Accordingly, choosing the cervical sympathetic as a sympathetic nerve easy of access, he divided that nerve in the neck. Holding the preconceived idea that the influence of the nerve, if any such existed, was in the direction of bringing about chemical changes involving the setting

VASO-MOTOR NERVES

free of heat, he expected to find that the section of the nerve by removing that influence would lead to a lowering of temperature. To his surprise he obtained a contrary result. When in a rabbit or other animal he divided the cervical sympathetic on one side of the neck, the temperature of that side of the head and neck, instead of falling, rose, the rise being, under favourable circumstances, very considerable, several degrees Centigrade, and readily appreciated even by the hand. A similar rise, or even a more marked one, followed the removal of the superior cervical ganglion on one side. At the same time he observed an increase in the sensibility of the side of the head operated on ; and the title of his first communication on the subject, read at the Société de Biologie in December, 1851, was "Influence du grand sympathique sur la

CLAUDE BERNARD

sensibilité et sur la calorification." A subsequent communication on the same subject to the Académie des Sciences on the 29th of March of the following year[1] bears a similar title, " De l'influence du système nerveux grand sympathique sur la chaleur animale." Not a word in the title of either paper about vascular effects. Yet in both papers, though they are very short, he describes the changes in the blood-vessels. In the latter he says, " All the part of the head which becomes hot after the section of the nerve becomes also the seat of a more active circulation. The arteries especially seem fuller and appear to pulsate more forcibly ; this is very distinctly seen, in the case of the rabbit, in the vessels of the ear." He reserves for further consideration the question " whether the vascular changes are the

[1] "Compt. Rend.," xxxiv. p. 472.

VASO-MOTOR NERVES

cause or the effect of the rise of temperature."

Bernard published the account of this experiment as a contribution to our knowledge of animal heat; but it will ever remain as the first clear and decided experimental proof of what we now call the vaso-motor functions of the nervous system. I say "the first clear and decided proof," for not only, as we have seen, had previous observers drawn inferences, chiefly from pathological phenomena, concerning the influence of nerves on the blood-vessels, but vascular changes had been observed in connection with the cervical sympathetic nerve itself. Thus so long before as 1727 Pourfour du Petit had observed redness of the conjunctiva in the dog after section of the cervical sympathetic, and the same effect had been noticed by subsequent observers, such as

CLAUDE BERNARD

Dupuy, Brachet, and John Reid. But the attention of these and other inquirers had been almost exclusively concentrated on the remarkable effects of the cervical sympathetic on the pupil ; in watching the constriction of the pupil which followed section of the cervical sympathetic, they neglected attendant phenomena. Even in the remarkable memoir by Budge and Waller, presented to the Académie des Sciences in the same year as that with which we are now dealing, 1851, in which the pupil-constricting fibres of the cervical sympathetic are traced to the spinal cord, and in preparing which the authors must have repeatedly come across the phenomena to which Bernard calls attention, there is nothing which can be considered as in any way forestalling Bernard's discovery. They were looking at the pupil and saw, so to speak, nothing else.

VASO-MOTOR NERVES

Indeed Bernard himself tells us that from the very beginning of his experimental studies in 1841, he had repeatedly divided the cervical sympathetic without observing the phenomena which he saw for the first time in 1851. In these previous experiments his attention, like that of others, had been directed to the pupil; it was not until the day that he looked for changes in the face and ear that he saw them. He was, it was true, looking for animal heat, but he saw also the vascular changes, saw them and spoke of them in such a way that never afterwards could they be ignored. With his experiment and not with any of those made by his forerunners does our knowledge of the influence of the nervous system on the blood-vessels really begin.

That Bernard's observation had the significance which we are claiming for it

CLAUDE BERNARD

is indeed clear from the fact that it immediately attracted great attention throughout the whole scientific world. Before August of the same year, 1852, the news of it had crossed the Atlantic, for we find Brown-Séquard, then sojourning in America, publishing in the *Philadelphia Medical Examiner* of that month, a paper in which the following words appear :—

" I have found that the remarkable phenomena which follow the section of the cervical part of the sympathetic, are mere consequences of the paralysis and therefore of the dilatation of the blood-vessels. The blood finding a larger way than usual, arrives there in greater quantity ; therefore the nutrition is more active. Now the sensibility is increased because the vital properties of the nerves are augmented when their nutrition is augmented. . . . I base my opinion in part

VASO-MOTOR NERVES

on the following experiments : If galvanism is applied to the superior portion of the sympathetic after it has been cut in the neck, the vessels of the face and of the ear after a certain time begin to contract; their contraction increases slowly, but at last it is evident that they resume their normal condition, if they are not even smaller. Then the temperature and the sensibility diminish in the face and in the ear, and they become in the palsied side the same as in the sound side. When the galvanic current ceases to act, the vessels begin to dilate again, and all the phenomena discovered by Dr. Bernard reappear."

Brown-Séquard thus supplied what we may call the second half of the vaso-motor proof; and it will be observed that he had none of Bernard's hesitation as to the interpretation of the phenomena. The rise of temperature as well as the increase of sensibility were to him simply the effects of the greater blood supply, due to the dilatation of the vessels.

A little later, in November of the same year, Bernard quite independently of and apparently in ignorance of Brown-Séquard's results made known [1] that galvanising the upper portion of the divided sympathetic produces effects diametrically opposed to those of section ; " the circulation from being active becomes feeble, the conjunctiva, the nostrils, and the ears, which were red, become pale." He therefore himself also supplied the second half of the vaso-motor proof.

Still a little later Waller, apparently ignorant alike of both Brown-Séquard's and Bernard's results, announced in a communication to the Académie des

[1] " C. R. Soc. Biol.," 1852, p. 168.

VASO-MOTOR NERVES

Sciences [1] that galvanism of the cervical sympathetic produced constriction of the blood-vessels of the head, and at the very same time Budge [2] showed that the fibres in the cervical sympathetic governing the blood-vessels, like the fibres for the pupil, took origin from the spinal cord.

Up to this time all Bernard's communications on the subject had been extremely brief, but in December 7th and 21st of 1853, he read a longer memoir before the Société de Biologie,[3] in which he more fully developed his views. It is worthy of note that though in the first section, historical in nature, of this paper, he states that he had shown that galvanism of the upper end of the divided cervical sym-

[1] " Compt. Rend.," 1853, xxxvi. p. 378, dated Feb., 1853.
[2] Ibid., p. 377.
[3] " Mémoires de la Soc. de Biol.," 1853, p. 77.

pathetic "caused all the troubles produced by the section of the nerve to disappear," he devotes the last and longest section to a discussion "on the relations which exist between the vascularisation and the calorification of the parts after the division of the great sympathetic." In this section, relying mainly on the fact that when the circulation in the ear is arrested by ligature of the two veins, the rise of temperature may still be observed upon division of the sympathetic, he argues that "the increased warmth cannot be explained by a pretended paralysis of the arteries which, by virtue of a passive enlargement allow a larger quantity of blood to circulate." And he insists on the fact, as indeed he did in his very first paper, that very often on the day after the section, though the vessels have returned to their normal condition, the rise of temperature per-

VASO-MOTOR NERVES

sists. "In a word," he concludes, "the vascular phenomenon which follows upon the section of the sympathetic nerve is active, not passive ; it is of the same nature as the vascular turgescence which occurs in a secreting organ on its passage from a condition of rest or of feeble activity to one of great activity."

Four years later, in a lecture at the Collége de France in June, 1857, he expounds the same views, employing at times the very words of his original communications ; he still maintains that the vascular phenomena cannot be referred "to a paralysis pure and simple of the arteries." In this lecture it may be remarked he insists, as indeed he had done in his earlier communications, that it is section of the sympathetic fibre alone which produces a rise of temperature, section of the sensory or motor fibre giving rise to a lowering of temperature; the rise of temperature which is observed after the section of a mixed nerve, such as the sciatic, is due to the sympathetic fibres present which have joined the nerve, peripheral to its spinal roots.

In Bernard's mind the importance of his experiments on the sympathetic lay in the proof which they afforded that the nervous system did act directly on the chemical changes in the tissues, and so intervened in the development of heat; the vascular phenomena he regarded as of secondary importance. Dwelling on the fact, which by that time had become to be regarded as established, that the warmth of the blood is supplied to it by the development of heat in the tissues through which it passes, rather than by generation of

VASO-MOTOR NERVES

heat in itself, and arguing that the tissues of the face, and even of the ear, contribute to the blood their quota of heat by virtue of the chemical changes going on in them, he was inclined to think that the tissue changes formed the primary object of the nerve supply, and that the vascular changes were rather the effect than the cause of the rise of temperature.

He was, however, himself soon led—and this is a marked instance of how always in his inquiries he conscientiously followed the teaching of his experimental facts in spite of his preconceived opinions—to furnish an instance in which chemical phenomena were obviously the result of the vascular changes, and at the same time to make the second great advance in our knowledge of the vaso-motor system.

In the very first scientific paper which he published, that in 1841, on the chorda tympani, Bernard had been led to deny that this nerve has any influence over the secretion of the submaxillary gland. In the very same year, 1851, that Bernard had discovered the vaso-motor functions of the sympathetic, Ludwig published his classical paper on the secretory functions of the chorda tympani. That great physiologist did not, however, observe, or at least did not describe, any of the attendant vascular phenomena.

In the January of 1858, Bernard, working on the submaxillary and other glands, announced to the Académie des Sciences[1] that when a gland is actively secreting, the blood which issues from it along the veins, is not as in the case of the blood issuing from an active muscle, dark in colour, but is bright red, in fact arterial. In the next month, in a short commu-

[1] "Compt. Rend.," xlvi. p. 159.

VASO-MOTOR NERVES

nication to the Société de Biologie [1] followed by a longer one in the succeeding August to the Académie des Sciences [2] he made known that this feature of the venous blood of the submaxillary gland only appeared as a result of stimulation of the chorda tympani nerve ; when the other nerve which supplied the gland, namely, the sympathetic, was stimulated, the venous blood issuing from the gland was dark, even darker than usual. The gland in fact was under the dominion of two kinds of nerves, the one giving rise on stimulation to a bright and the other to a dark venous blood, the flow in the former case being full and rapid, in the latter scanty and slow. He showed that the same phenomena of two antagonistic nerves might be observed in other glands ; and he sup-

[1] "Compt. Rend. de la Soc. d. Biol.," 1858, p. 29. [2] "Compt. Rend.," xlvii. p. 245.

plied the true explanation of the phenomena. He argued that the bright red arterial colour of the venous blood issuing from the gland upon stimulation of the chorda and the dark colour of the same blood when the sympathetic is stimulated could not be due to the direct action of the nerves on the blood ; " there must be intermediate conditions, and these are supplied by the different mechanical modifications brought about in the capillary circulation by the two nerves respectively." The chorda tympani dilates the vessels, and brings about so rapid a circulation that the blood has not time to lose its arterial colour in passing through the capillaries. The sympathetic constricts the vessels, impedes and slackens the flow, and so permits the gaseous exchange to be exaggerated. "The sympathetic nerve is the constrictor nerve of the blood-vessels ; the

VASO-MOTOR NERVES

tympanico-lingual (chorda tympani) is their dilatator."

This is the first announcement, this is the statement of the discovery, of vaso-constrictor and vaso-dilator nerves.

To Claude Bernard, then, we owe the foundations of our knowledge of the vaso-motor system. He made known to us the existence of vaso-motor nerves, and he also made known to us that vaso-motor nerves are of two kinds, vaso-constrictor and vaso-dilator. These are the two fundamental facts of vaso-motor physiology ; all else supplied by many others is built up on these.

It is also worthy of note, as indicative of the spirit of the true inquirer, that Bernard came upon both these truths while he was in each case looking for something else. In his research on the sympathetic, his mind was fastened on the relation of the

CLAUDE BERNARD

nerves to animal heat ; in his research on the submaxillary gland he was trying to make out the differences in the colour of the venous blood according as the gland was active or at rest. In each case he had the genius to appreciate the value of the new truths which thus incidentally, as it were, came to the surface. A more ordinary observer, with his mind bent solely on his main theme, might have neglected these so to speak side issues. It was Bernard's characteristic, and the secret of his success as an inquirer, that he was ever ready to turn aside and grasp a truth thus presenting itself by the way.

Though Bernard admitted, and indeed himself supplied the mechanical explanation of the change in colour of the blood as the mere result of the widening or narrowing of the arteries, he never even up to the end abandoned the position which he had

VASO-MOTOR NERVES

at the first taken up, that the rise of temperature which follows section of the sympathetic fibres is not to be explained as the mere result of the fuller rush of blood through the widened blood-vessels. He insisted to the last, that there was, or that there might be, a direct action of the nerve on the tissues changes which formed the local source of heat. In his " Leçons sur la chaleur animale," delivered in 1872, but published in 1876, little more than a year before his death, we find expressions of his views on this question cropping up from time to time. Thus, p. 222, " The calorific phenomena depend on actions of two kinds, on a vascular action and on a concomitant chemical action." Again, p. 288, " The nervous system seems at first sight to bring about calorification only by the intervention of the circulation. It is to a vasomotor action alone that one at first refers

CLAUDE BERNARD

the modification of animal heat. Although this may be true to a certain extent, we cannot, however, consider it as an adequate cause, we cannot refuse to admit an action of the sympathetic different from a purely vaso-motor action, an action which has for a result a local increase of activity in the chemical changes of the tissues attended by a direct production of heat. It is not only by dilating the vessels, by increasing the local circulation, by bathing the tissues more fully with hot blood, that the section of the sympathetic brings about a rise of temperature; it acts also by increasing the local combustions or chemical metabolism. The vaso-motor action is accompanied by a chemical action on the nutrition of the tissues. . . . Conversely, it is not only because it constricts the blood-vessels that the galvanisation of the sympathetic produces cold, it is because it checks and

VASO-MOTOR NERVES

slows at the same time the chemical movement of nutrition. So long as one looks upon the lowering of temperature as the result simply of the constriction of the vessels, one may confine oneself to speaking of the sympathetic as a constrictor nerve of the blood-vessels. But if one admits, as I do, the independence of the two effects, a special name is wanted for each. One must say that, apart from its vaso-motor action, the sympathetic exerts a thermic influence. Stimulation of it produces a frigorific effect; section or paralysis of it produces a calorific effect. It is not only a constrictor nerve of the vessels, it is also a frigorific nerve." Again, p. 443, dealing with fever he says: " The phenomena of nutrition are of two kinds : the one kind is that of destruction, of splitting up, of material disorganisation or combustion ; the other is of organisation or organic synthesis." The latter phenomena are under the influence of frigorific nerves which belong more especially to the sympathetic system ; the phenomena of combustion are more specially governed by the vaso-dilator or calorific nerves which belong more particularly to the cerebro-spinal system. " Now fever is essentially an exaggeration of the action of the calorific nerves and not merely a paralysis of the vaso-constrictor nerves."

It is almost impossible to exaggerate the importance of these labours of Bernard on the vaso-motor nerves, since it is almost impossible to exaggerate the influence which our knowledge of the vaso-motor system, springing as it does from Bernard's researches as from its fount and origin, has exerted, is exerting, and in widening measure will continue to exert, on all our physiological and pathological conceptions, on medical practice, and on the conduct

VASO-MOTOR NERVES

of human life. There is hardly a physiological discussion of any width in which we do not sooner or later come upon vasomotor questions. Whatever part of physiology we touch, be it the work done by a muscle, be it the various kinds of secretive labour, be it the insurance of the brain's well-being in the midst of the hydrostatic vicissitudes to which the change of daily life subject it, be it that maintenance of bodily temperature which is a condition of the body's activity : in all these, as in many other things, we find vaso-motor factors intervening. And if, passing the insecure and wavering line which parts health from illness, we find ourselves dealing with inflammation or with fever, or with any of the disordered physiological processes which constitute disease, we shall find, whatever be the tissue specially affected by the morbid conditions, that vaso-motor

CLAUDE BERNARD

influences have to be taken into account. The idea of vaso-motor action is woven as a dominant thread into all the physiological and pathological doctrines of to-day ; attempt to draw out that thread and all that would be left would appear as a tangled heap.

All this dominant knowledge has come, as does a full stream from the spring which is its source, from Bernard's initial experiment on the cervical sympathetic. This is one of not a few instances, in which a simple experiment on a living animal, has brought suddenly a great light in a field where men had been groping in vain with the help of mere clinical observations. Before this simple experiment attention had again and again been drawn to cases in which there seemed to be some connection between vascular changes and affections or conditions of nerves; but in none of these did there come to light any clear teaching as to what that connection really was; all was uncertain and obscure. The result of the experiment was the first clear light which broke upon the subject; and it was the following up of the teaching of the experiment which supplied the interpretation of the hitherto obscure clinical facts.

And it may be well here to insist that the experiment in question was what is called a vivisectional experiment—an experiment which Bernard, had he lived in this country and in our day, might have been prevented from doing; his work might thus have been strangled at its very birth. Some, in whom sentiment is stronger than knowledge, are fond of declaring that all such experiments are useless and needless, since the knowledge gained by them might be come at in other ways. The unbiassed inquirer in the genesis of scientific truths and conceptions may be ready to admit that in the course of time experiments of Nature's making, not of man's, might have suggested to some quick mind that nerve-fibres act on blood-vessels, and might even have hinted how they act. And haply to the same quick mind, or to others following after him, duly impressed with what had been thus suggested, there might afterwards at some time or other, by fortunate occurrence, have come other like experiments of Nature confirming the suggestion and establishing it as a proved truth. The unbiassed inquirer will admit this ; but he will also acknowledge that up to the day of Bernard's experiment all the experiments which a seemingly cruel Nature had carried out year after year, and day after

VASO-MOTOR NERVES

day, on suffering mankind and suffering animals, passed before the eyes of observer after observer, quick to see and eager to note, without suggesting anything more than the dimmest and shadowest ideas of such an action of nerve-fibre on blood-vessel. And he will also admit that one stroke of Bernard's knife — a stroke bringing a pain which shrinks to a vanishing point compared with the pain which it has been the means to spare— laid bare a truth, which all Nature's cruel strokes had during long years been unable to bring to light.

During the latter half of the century which is drawing to its close, the power of the healer to cure or lessen disease, and to prevent or soften pain, has grown with a swiftness which is in a measure marvellous, and that in spite of the great helplessness which is still all too often witnessed. That power is, as we have just said, in part the outcome of truer, wider views of vaso-motor action; and whatever we may say about the might have been, there remains the plain historical fact that those wider, truer views have had their origin in Bernard's initial experiment on a living animal.

VI

OTHER DISCOVERIES

THE discoveries of glycogen, of vasomotor nerves, and of the action of the pancreatic juice form Bernard's greatest claims to fame; but he also enriched physiology with a large number of results, of value less than that of any of the above, though of varied importance. We need dwell on two or three of these only.

In the quite early years of his career he just missed the opportunity of associating his name with a discovery, the influence of which on the progress of physiology has been not much less than that of the

CLAUDE BERNARD

discovery of glycogen or that of the discovery of vaso-motor nerves.

If the views accepted and expounded by physiologists at the present time, especially perhaps those relating to the actions taking place within the central nervous system, be analysed, it will be found that the doctrine of inhibition plays a very important part. It is not less dominant, it is perhaps even more dominant, in pathological views, and in the application of physiology to medical practice. Now the doctrine of inhibition had its origin in an experiment made known by the brothers Ernst Heinrich and Eduard Friedrich Weber orally, at Naples, in the fall of 1845, and by means of print in 1846; the experiment, namely (now so well known), of the stoppage of the heart's beat by stimulation of the vagus nerve. That experiment, which still remains the typical inhibition experiment,

OTHER DISCOVERIES

was the first clear proof that a nervous impulse, instead of giving rise as in many, and indeed in ordinary cases, it does, to an expenditure of energy, may check expenditure and by banking up energy increase in this tissue or in that the potential store. It has been the starting-point of a clearer insight into the molecular changes of the tissues, and into the mode of working of the nervous system.

Now in 1846, in the very same year in which the brothers Weber published their discovery, Bernard had quite independently come upon the same result. He himself tells us [1] that in that year he ausculted a dog while the vagus nerve was being stimulated, and that he "observed with the greatest ease that at every galvanisation the heart stopped and the sound ceased, recurring again so soon

[1] " Leçons sur le système nerveux," ii. p. 381.

CLAUDE BERNARD

as the galvanism was removed." He mentioned the result in his private courses, and it was published by one of his pupils, a Dr. Lefèvre, in a thesis which appeared in 1848.

But Bernard never grasped the real bearing of the result which he thus observed. Though he returned to the subject in a communication to the Société de Biologie in 1849 [1] he never followed it up; and indeed, though in his lectures on the nervous system, as well as in his later writings, he expounds or refers to the facts of inhibition, these never seem to have largely or deeply occupied his thoughts, never tempted him on to speculations as to the nature and mode of action of inhibition, such as have largely exercised the minds of many German and other physiologists. Indeed, so

[1] "C. R. de la Soc. de Biol.," 1849, p. 13.

OTHER DISCOVERIES

late as 1858, he speaks of the stoppage of the heart by the vagus as "a singular experiment of which several interpretations and explanations have been offered."

Bernard was very early attracted to the study of poisons. He recognised in them, as he himself has said, physiological instruments of greater delicacy than the mechanical means at the disposal of the physiologist, instruments capable of analysing, of dissecting as it were, the anatomical elements of the body while this is yet alive. He looked upon them as true "vital reagents." Studying them from this point of view, rather than with the desire to compile the complete toxicological or physiological history of any one of them, he was, on the one hand, led to important general physiological conclusions, and, on the other

CLAUDE BERNARD

hand, enriched his science with valuable new methods of inquiry. His success in this direction was conspicuous in the case of curare and carbonic monoxide.

Curare, otherwise spelt as urari, and in many other ways, an arrow poison of the South American Indians, was first brought to Europe by Sir W. Raleigh from Guiana in 1595. It had been described by many authors, its botanical origin and its general chemical features had been studied, and several authors including Brodie the great English surgeon, and Charles Waterton, the traveller, had experimented with it. But Bernard was the first to analyse with accuracy its physiological action.

He tells us that in 1844 he received from his friend Pelouze, a supply of the poison, being some which Goudat had brought over from Brazil, and immediately began to experiment with it. He did not, how-

OTHER DISCOVERIES

ever, publish anything of the results which he had obtained until 1850, in which year he made a communication to the Académie des Sciences on October 15 [1] and to the Société de Biologie in December.[2] In the former longer paper he hardly says more than that the poison kills rapidly without convulsions and at once renders the nerves inexcitable; he does not distinguish between different kinds of nerves, in respect to its action; and indeed the greater part of the paper is taken up in showing that the poison does not diffuse from the interior of the alimentary canal into the blood, and hence is harmless when swallowed, though a minute quantity introduced into a wound is rapidly fatal. In the second communication he says that the poison abolishes reflex actions, destroying rapidly

[1] "Compt. Rend.," xxxi. p. 533.
[2] "C. R. de la Soc. de Biol.," 1850, p. 195.

and completely the motor and sensory properties of the nervous system; and he especially insists that, while it at once renders the nerves inexcitable, it leaves the muscles fully excitable, in this respect affording a marked contrast to nicotine, which destroys the irritability of the muscles and in causing death brings about convulsions. This marked effect on the nerves in the absence of any effect on the muscles was recognised by Bernard, and perhaps even more distinctly by others, as a convincing proof of the correctness of the view that the irritability which muscular tissue displays is an independent property of its own, and not merely one conferred on it by the nervous tissue supplying it, a matter which at the time served as the occasion of lively controversy.

From 1850 to 1856, Bernard published no formal account of the researches

OTHER DISCOVERIES

which he continued to make on curare, but from his paper communicated to the Académie des Sciences in 1856 [1] as well as from his "Leçons sur les effets des substances toxiques," published in 1857, we learn that already in 1852 he had arrived at and made known, apparently in his lectures at the Collége de France, further remarkable results, which in the succeeding years he continued to extend and complete.

In 1852, having observed that the muscles of a frog poisoned with curare so far from being less irritable, seemed to be more irritable, than normal muscles, and being aware that the individual differences existing between frogs rendered the comparison of the muscles of one frog with those of another more or less inexact, and at least inconclusive, he was led to make a

[1] "Compt. Rend.," xliii. p. 825.

CLAUDE BERNARD

comparative experiment on the muscles of one and the same animal, by tying the blood-vessels of one leg, so as to shut off the blood stream from the tissues of that leg before he introduced the curare into the circulation. He found his views corroborated; the muscles in the leg supplied with blood and so with poison, were more irritable to direct electric stimulation and remained so for a longer time than did the muscles in the leg from which the blood and therefore the poison had been cut off by the ligature. But in making the experiment his attention was arrested by another fact, that the leg, protected from the curare by the ligature not only remained sensitive, so that it was moved when it was stimulated, but also that movements took place in it when the skin in the parts of the body to which the poison had had access were stimulated;

OTHER DISCOVERIES

that is to say, stimulation of the skin, which produced no reflex action in the poisoned moiety of the body, could bring about by reflex action movements of the muscles in the unpoisoned leg. He at once grasped the meaning of this, namely, that while motor nerves were rendered inactive by the poisons, the sensory nerves and the central nervous system remained intact. Here again we have an instance of how Bernard's genius led him to turn aside from an inquiry which he had begun in order to follow up a hint which, as it were, accidentally presented itself. When he made the experiment his mind was wholly directed towards the influence of curare upon the muscles; but he at once left these to seize upon the new fact concerning nerves, which had always escaped him in his previous observations. By similarly devised experiments, now the common demonstrational experiments of the lecture room and the laboratory, he supplied proof that curare acts upon the motor nerves, the abolition of their functions being peripheral, not central, and that not only the motor nerves to the skeletal muscles, but other efferent nerves, such as the vagus fibres to the heart, are by an adequate dose of the poison similarly paralysed.

This fundamental fact he had observed so early as 1852, but in this case as in so many others he did not rush forward to publish it. In contrast to many of his own time and since he had a dread of making known any new result, however important and sure it might seem, until he had had opportunity to work the matter thoroughly out. Indeed he complains of how against his will he at times gave to the world a discovery in an unfinished condition, because the insufficiency

OTHER DISCOVERIES

of his laboratory and of other means of experimenting left him no hope of perfecting it as he desired. " I am only too familiar with the regrets of the investigator who, simply by reason of the lack of material means is prevented from carrying out the experiments which he has devised, and is driven to abandon researches which he has in his head and is led to make known a discovery while it is as yet a mere rough sketch, not a completed work."[1] It was not until 1856 that he gave a formal account of what he had discovered four years before; and he was led to speak then because Kölliker at Würzburg, in that year published a paper showing that he had independently arrived at the same main results. The priority however clearly belongs to Bernard, though Kölliker's investigation was in some respects more complete and

[1] " Physiologie générale," p. 209.

CLAUDE BERNARD

exact. Since then curare has become an instrument in the hands of the physiologist of the same order as that supplied by anæsthetics ; by enabling him to abolish temporarily the movements of the skeletal muscles it has enabled him to carry out observations which could not have been made at all or could not have been made satisfactorily without such aid. And the knowledge which has thus been gained is indirectly due to Bernard.

In many of the instances in which in his writings Bernard has dwelt on the action of curare, he has in an almost dramatic manner insisted upon its leaving intact the sensory elements of the nervous system. And indeed there is every reason to believe that with a certain dose of the poison an animal may be killed without its sensations being affected until the nervous system is poisoned not by the drug

OTHER DISCOVERIES

but by the blood ceasing to be oxygenated owing to the paralysis of the respiratory pump. But Bernard himself came to recognise that the exact limits of the action of the poison were largely determined by the dose, that while a small quantity in the blood at any one time affected only the motor nerves of the skeletal muscles, a larger quantity interfered also with the vaso-motor nerves; and Kölliker was nearer the truth than Bernard when, even in his first communication, he maintained that the poison could act on the central nervous system and so affect sensation if present in the blood in adequate quantity.

Of hardly less value than his work on curare was Bernard's analysis of the physiological (poisonous) action of carbonic monoxide gas. The extremely poisonous nature, even in small quantity, of this gas, so apt

CLAUDE BERNARD

to appear when combustion, as in stoves, is imperfect, had long been known ; as had also the fact that though death through it seems to be a kind of " suffocation," the blood, during the poisoning and after death is not as in ordinary suffocation dark, almost black, but bright red in colour, as bright or even brighter than ordinary arterial blood. But how the gas acted, and how it caused death, was unknown until Bernard took up the matter. In respect to this also, as to curare, he had solved the problem some time before he formally announced the solution. His formal communication to the Académie des Sciences was not made until September, 1858 ;[1] but he there says that he had made his first observations ten years before and had expounded his conclusions in his lectures of 1853, and again in those of 1856.

[1] "Compt. Rend.," xlvii. p. 393.

OTHER DISCOVERIES

Indeed a brief account of these appears in Atlee's notes of his lectures, published in Philadelphia in 1854; and he himself included a somewhat fuller description of his results in his "Leçons sur les effets des substances toxiques," published in 1857. In any case he had solved the problem before 1857, and the value of that solution will be apparent if the state of knowledge concerning the gases of the blood be kept in mind.

Lavoisier, in making known the fundamental truth that the central fact of respiration is the disappearance of a certain quantity of oxygen from the inspired, and the appearance of a certain quantity of carbonic acid in the expired air, had, at the beginning of the century, propounded the further view that the oxygen goes and the carbonic comes in consequence of a subtle substance contain-

CLAUDE BERNARD

ing carbon and oxygen being secreted from the blood into the air passages and being there oxidised. This view, though it came to be regarded as years went on with increasing doubt, was not wholly abandoned until Magnus in 1838 published his researches on the gases of the blood. Those researches marked an epoch in the Theory of Respiration. Magnus showed that both arterial and venous blood contained both oxygen and carbonic acid, that arterial blood contained more oxygen and less carbonic acid than did venous, and that respiration consisted in the blood gaining oxygen and losing carbonic acid in the lungs, and losing oxygen and gaining carbonic acid in the tissues. That was a great step ; but Magnus maintained that both gases were simply dissolved in the blood, the quantity of each present

OTHER DISCOVERIES

being determined by the law of pressures. This view held its position for many years. Though contested by Liebig, it was the dominant view at the time Bernard began the observations with which we are dealing. Not until after he had arrived at the conclusion of which we are about to speak, namely in 1857, were Magnus's views overthrown by observations carried out by L. Meyer on Magnus's lines, but leading to the conclusion that the gases of the blood are not wholly present as merely dissolved gases, but exist in some loose unstable combination from which they can, under appropriate circumstances, be set free. This Meyer very distinctly showed to be the condition of the oxygen in the blood, but he failed to discover the substance or substances in the blood with which it so combined. The red corpuscles were suspected to

CLAUDE BERNARD

be concerned in the matter; but though crystals, of what we now call hæmoglobin had been described by Reichert, Funke and others, hæmatin was still spoken of as the colouring matter of the blood, and all Meyer's attempts to connect with hæmatin the absorption of oxygen by the blood failed. Our knowledge on this matter was not put on a proper footing until Hoppe (Hoppe-Seyler) in 1862 and Stokes in 1864 published their spectroscopic observations.

Meanwhile, before 1857, Bernard had got at the truth by help of carbonic monoxide. He had certainly made the fundamental experiments in 1855, and according to his own account had already made some of them in 1848, having observed the peculiar colour of the blood in carbonic monoxide poisoning so early

OTHER DISCOVERIES

as 1842, at the very beginning almost of his career.

He observed that blood taken from the right side of the heart in animals poisoned by carbonic oxide and exposed to an atmosphere containing, like ordinary air, a known quantity of oxygen, did not, as did normal blood, take up oxygen. He further observed that when normal blood was exposed to an atmosphere of carbonic monoxide it gave up oxygen at the same time that it absorbed carbonic monoxide, and that the volumes of oxygen so given up and carbonic monoxide so absorbed were equal. Reflecting that the different colours of arterial and venous blood must be due to the behaviour of the red corpuscles in relation to the gases of the two kinds of blood, he jumped, as it were, to the conclusion that the red corpuscles were concerned in the retention both of

CLAUDE BERNARD

oxygen and carbonic oxide by the blood. This was confirmed by the further observation that the beneficial effects of the transfusion of blood, which are obviously due to the red corpuscles, since serum free from corpuscles has no such effects, were absent when the blood used was carbonic monoxide blood. This gave him the key to an understanding of the way in which carbonic monoxide poisons the animal body. "I was thus led," says he, "to find that this gas rapidly poisons animals, because it instantly displaces the oxygen of the red corpuscles and cannot itself be subsequently displaced by oxygen." " The animal dies because the red corpuscles are, as it were, paralysed and circulate as inert bodies devoid of the power of sustaining life."

Some of the details of the experiments on which Bernard based this view may be

OTHER DISCOVERIES

open to criticism, but it remains nevertheless true that by these researches he secured a threefold gain. He explained the mode of action of carbonic oxide, and so opened the way for rational remedial measures. He introduced an easy and ready method of measuring the quantity of available respiratory oxygen in any given quantity of blood, a method which, both in his own hands and in those of others, has proved of great service. And, by a sort of inspiration, he anticipated the conclusions arrived at in a more laborious way by his German brethren, and reached, almost in one step, a correct view of the nature of the respiratory process. This view, moreover, assisted by the method, enabled him to push forward his inquiries into the functions and behaviour of the blood as the great "internal medium" on which the tissues live, and thus incidentally led him, as we have seen, to the discovery of the distinction between vaso-constrictor and vaso-motor nerves.

There are many other results which Bernard arrived at, such as the so-called paralytic secretion, the supposed reflex activity of the sympathetic ganglia, and others; but on these we need not dwell in detail, though they are often quoted in physiological literature.

One observation of his, however, perhaps deserves notice. In the "fifties" biologists, especially perhaps in France, were engaged in a fierce controversy about spontaneous generation, a controversy laid to rest in the main by Pasteur, and now well nigh forgotten. To that controversy Bernard made a notable contribution in 1858.[1] He showed that the growths which readily appear in a solution con-

[1] "Ann. d. Sc. Nat.," ix., 1858, p. 360.

OTHER DISCOVERIES

taining gelatine and dextrose exposed to the air, do not appear if the solution be supplied exclusively with air which has passed through a red-hot tube. He argued that the growths which usually appear are not spontaneous in origin but have their source in air-borne germs, and the red-hot tubes killed the germs on their way to the solution. Much of Pasteur's refutation of the spontaneous generation theory was on the lines of Bernard's experiment.

VII

His Later Writings

FROM the preceding chapters it will be seen that all, or nearly all, Bernard's great achievements were accomplished during that period of his life which ended with the year 1860. Looking more closely we may see that the essential results of his two greatest discoveries, the glycogenic function of the liver and the vasomotor system, were gained so early as about 1850, within the first ten years of his career as an investigator.

The great truths, which it was given to him to lay bare, were not reached by the help of easy circumstances and ample

HIS LATER WRITINGS

opportunities for inquiry such as fall to the lot of at least most of the young men of science of to-day. I am not speaking of the attendant difficulties of earning the daily bread; these are known, perhaps one may say happily known, to almost all young inquirers of all times. I am contrasting Bernard's surroundings at the commencement of his career with those of the young man who at the present time desires to devote himself to scientific research. The latter, at least in most cases, finds in some way or other access to a well-furnished laboratory, in which the path of investigation is made smooth, perhaps in some cases too smooth, for him, in which adequate apparatus is placed at his disposal, and in which he is at once trained in the technique of inquiry and guided in his thoughts by the sympathetic and suggestive words of a wise and experienced master.

CLAUDE BERNARD.

None of these things came to Bernard. He had, it is true, encouragement and an example in Magendie, but hardly more; and even this was not much. So far as example went, beyond a strenuous desire to put everything to the test of experiment, there was little of intellectual training which Magendie could impart to Bernard. Indeed, it could not have been long before the pupil began to feel, as the stronger man of the two, his natural enthusiasm for his master checked by a growing conviction that the master's hand was often pointing the wrong way. Nor in the details of experimental execution was there much for Bernard to learn; indeed, it was for the most part the other way. After the third or fourth lecture, at which Bernard assisted as *préparateur*, Magendie, struck with the superb skill with which Bernard had conducted the lecture demonstrations, said, in his usual gruff way, as he left the lecture-room at the close of the lecture, " You are a better man than I am."

In the way of material advantages for research Magendie had little to offer to his assistant. As Bernard himself (" Physiologie générale," p. 203) has told us, experimental physiology was then looked down upon. Natural history was in the ascendant. Botany, zoology, and geology had their museums. The great and dominant Cuvier mocked at experiments on living animals, maintaining that they were simply sources of erroneous views. Chemistry was rising fast and was being provided with adequate laboratories. But for physiology nothing was being done. On the contrary, it was being persecuted and reviled. " In those days the physiologist had need of a real passion for his

CLAUDE BERNARD

science, and in order to ward off fatal discouragement had to possess his soul of high courage and great patience. So soon as an experimental physiologist was discovered he was denounced ; he was given over to the reproaches of his neighbours and subjected to annoyances by the police."

In the Collége de France, devoted though it was to scientific inquiry, no better place as a laboratory was found for Magendie than a corner, spoken of as "a damp and dark lair," a hiding-place for a wild beast. And Bernard himself has said : "I had ample opportunity, while I served as his assistant, to note the continual obstacles which the administration of the college put in his way."

It was not in Magendie's power to offer his assistant opportunities for research, and Bernard, even after his appointment to the

HIS LATER WRITINGS

assistantship, had to carry on his experimental inquiries in some temporary laboratory of his own, or in that of one of his chemical friends, such as in that of Pelouze. We have already (p. 12) said something of the circumstances amid which he made his first researches; and the following story which he tells in his "Physiologie générale," illustrates the nomadic character of his experimental installations, and the difficulties amid which he prosecuted his early inquiries.

"About 1844 I was studying the digestive powers of gastric juice by the help of the method introduced by Blondlot, namely, that of collecting gastric juice by means of a cannula, or sort of silver tap, fitted into the stomach of a live dog in such a way that the health of the animal does not in the least suffer thereby. Just then the celebrated surgeon of Berlin,

[marginalia: Gastric work on dogs.]

Dieffenbach, was on a visit to Paris ; and, hearing of my experiments through my friend Pelouze, he was anxious to witness the operation of the introduction of the gastric cannula. Informed of his wish, I hastened to gratify it, and performed the experiment on a dog in the chemical laboratory which Pelouze then had in the Rue Dauphine. After the operation the animal was shut up in the yard of the laboratory in order that we might examine it again later on. But on the morrow it was found that the dog had, in spite of precautions, escaped, carrying still in its belly the accusing cannula of a physiologist. Some days afterwards, quite early in the morning, before I had got up, I was visited by a person who came to tell me that the police commissioner of the quarter of the École-de-Médecine wanted to speak with me, and requested me to call on him. In the course of the day I presented myself at the police office in the Rue du Jardinet. I found there a little old man of a very respectable appearance, who received me very coldly, and at first said nothing. Then, taking me into an adjoining room, he showed me, to my great astonishment, the dog on which I had operated in Pelouze's laboratory, and asked me if I admitted having placed in the dog the instrument which he had in his belly. I replied in the affirmative, adding that I was delighted to find my cannula again, for I had given it up as lost. My answer, however, instead of satisfying the commissioner, appeared to anger him, for he addressed to me an admonition couched in the severest terms, accompanied by threats at my audacity in having taken his dog to experiment on. I explained that it was

not I who had taken his dog, but that I
had bought it of the men who were in the
habit of selling dogs to the physiologists,
and who stated that they were employed
by the police to collect stray dogs. I
added that I regretted having been the
involuntary cause of the pain which the
misfortune of his dog had caused him,
that the animal would not die of it, and
that there was only one thing to do,
namely, to let me take back my silver
cannula and for him to keep the dog.
These last words at once made the commissioner change his manner of speaking,
and completely appeased his wife and
daughter. I removed my instrument,
and on leaving promised to call again.
And, indeed, I visited the Rue du Jardinet
several times. In a few days the dog was
completely cured, I became a friend of
the commissioner, and could henceforward

HIS LATER WRITINGS

count on his protection. Indeed this led me to establish my laboratory within his district ; and for some years, until, in fact, I was appointed deputy to Magendie at the Collége de France, I was enabled to continue my private courses of experimental physiology under the licence and protection of the commissioner, whereby I was saved many disagreeable incidents."

In 1847 Magendie's increasing infirmities led to Bernard's being appointed his Deputy at the Collége de France, and a career now seemed to be secured to him. He could henceforward work in an official laboratory ; and it was, as we have seen, during the succeeding few years that his most brilliant work was done.

Yet in 1851, at the very time that he was unlocking the gates of Fame, conscious though he must have been of the high value of the truths which he was beginning to make known, he was despairing of the future. The path of the experimental physiologist seemed so doubtful, the difficulties so many and so pressing, the hopes of success so few and so shadowy, that he at this time had serious thoughts of abandoning a career of science, and of devoting himself to active practice as a surgeon. His domestic relations probably had much to do with his discouragement; for he had, unhappily, married a wife who was in no way a helpmeet to him. Hers was a nature too commonplace to rise to any sympathy with his intellectual aspirations; she was not prepared, as he was, to live laborious days on narrow means, in order that the world might be the richer for the truths which he by patient toil might reap. She desired that the ability, which she learned from those around her gave promise of

HIS LATER WRITINGS

being of the kind which men call genius, should find immediate reward in that " which all women admire," and should change hardships and self-denials into ease and affluence. She thought that the life of a successful practitioner, riding to-day in his carriage and to-morrow forgotten, was far more to be desired than the life of a student whose present lay in obscurity, and whose future could not be foretold.

Happily Bernard had in him that which armed him against the temptation to leave the plough to which he had put his hand. When in 1847 he gave his first lecture as deputy for Magendie, he began with these words : "Scientific medicine, gentlemen, which it ought to be my duty to teach here, does not exist." He said this knowing that he who was speaking had both the ideas and the skill to realise those ideas, such as would go far to create the

CLAUDE BERNARD

lacking science. With this consciousness of his power he could not but go on. Nor had he long to wait before assurance came to him that he was not mistaken as to the path which he had marked out for himself. Whispers ran round among the Olympians of science that a young physiologist was doing remarkable work, whispers which soon strengthened into loud voices of unstinted praise. And speech was before long followed by action. Magendie still lingering on, Bernard's position at the Collége de France was the insecure and insufficient one of a mere deputy, whose term of office was dependent on the life of another. Recognising this, and recognising also that the physiology which Bernard was advancing and expounding, was not a mere technical adjunct to the art of medicine, but was of the kind which claimed to be considered as a branch of

HIS LATER WRITING

knowledge, of value for its own sake as a constituent part of philosophy, the authorities created in the faculty of Science of the University of Paris, at the Sorbonne, a new chair of General Physiology, and placed him in it as the first occupant. Though the post carried with it neither laboratory nor assistants, it at least gave Bernard an honourable position. Further recognition came in the same year in the form of election into the Academy of Medicine and Surgery, in succession to the great surgeon Roux. And in 1855, upon the death of Magendie, Bernard was without hesitation called to the vacant chair and made full Professor at the Collège de France. Henceforward there could be no question of his turning back from science.

During the next few years his activity was enormous. He extended and completed his great discoveries, and within

CLAUDE BERNARD

seventeen years from the beginning of his career as an inquirer, while he was as yet some three years short of fifty years of age, he had brought to the science for the sake of which he had deserted literature, all the wealth of riches on which we have dwelt in preceding chapters. At the same time he.was delivering lectures both at the Collége de France and at the Sorbonne, a course of forty lectures a year in each place. These lectures were no deliverances of academic platitudes, no formal expositions of acknowledged doctrines, composed once for all, and that without great labour, and repeated with but little change year after year. At the Collége de France, as we have seen, his hand was free; he could lecture on what he liked and how he liked. At the Sorbonne, the regulations for the chair prescribed lectures of a more didactic kind;

HIS LATER WRITINGS

but Bernard, ignoring the regulations, lectured there also in the way which he thought best, and no one gainsayed him. In both places he chose some subject for a course, and treated it as an inquiry, to be developed as the course went on by the help, not only of old, but also of new experiments. Each course which he gave was as a mere course a burden to him; he took no pleasure in exposition, this indeed was only weariness to him; it was inquiry, and inquiry alone, which satisfied his soul. In fact, he largely used his lectures as a means of making known new results and new or corrected and extended views. In many instances the communication in which he made known some new result to the Académie des Sciences or to the Société de Biologie, seems all too brief and imperfect, in fact, sometimes almost bald. One has to look to the published Leçons, in which the

CLAUDE BERNARD

matter is more fully treated of, in order to get the author's fuller exposition and to learn his more mature view. Many of Bernard's results, indeed, can only be found in these Leçons, and it is to these that we have to look for an adequate exposition of many of his ideas. Conscientiously reported by one or other of his talented pupils, and carefully revised by his own hand, the series of lectures thus delivered and published constitute Bernard's great contribution to physiological literature.

In these he developed more fully his views on the questions involved in his own researches, and his conceptions of general physiological truths. Taken together they constitute his testament in which may be found at once an account of his own labours, an exposition of the aims and methods of physiology, and a vindication

HIS LATER WRITINGS

of the value of the science to which he devoted his life.

The series begins with the " Leçons de Physiologie expérimentale," the first volume of which, published in 1855, contains the course delivered at the Collége de France in the winter of 1854–55, and deals chiefly with the physiology of sugar and with the glycogenic function of the liver, while the second volume which was published in the next year is devoted to digestion, and includes an account of the new results about the pancreas.

Next followed, in 1857, the "Leçons sur les effets des substances toxiques et médicamenteuses," delivered in 1856, also at the Collége de France, in which he, as we have seen, expounded his views on the action of curare and carbonic monoxide, though dwelling also on strychnine, nicotine,

CLAUDE BERNARD

ether, and other chemical substances. The dominant idea of the book is to develope the value of a drug as a means of physiological analysis.

In the next year, 1858, he published his " Leçons sur la physiologie et la pathologie du système nerveux," delivered at the Collége de France in the winter of 1856-57. The first volume is of the nature of a general exposition, though three lectures are devoted to the diabetic puncture; the second deals with the physiology of the several cranial nerves, with which, as the pupil of Magendie, Bernard was thoroughly conversant, and on which he himself had worked; and the last two lectures constitute an exposition of the new views as to the sympathetic nerve.

In 1859, appeared in two volumes the " Leçons sur les propriétés physiologiques et les altérations pathologiques des liquides de l'organisme," in which developing his pregnant idea of the blood as the "internal medium" on which the tissues live, he discoursed of the physiology of that and other fluids of the body in health and in disease. These seven volumes of lectures, all delivered at the Collége de France, he some years later formally presented to the Academy of Sciences.

They were followed in turn by the "Leçons de pathologie expérimentale," "Leçons sur les anesthétiques et sur l'asphyxie," "Leçons sur la chaleur animale," "Leçons sur le diabète," "Leçons sur les phénomènes de la vie," and lastly by the "Leçons de Physiologie opératoire." They form altogether 17 octavo volumes. He who reads the whole series consecutively will naturally come upon much repetition, especially in the exposition of ideas; but that is insepar-

CLAUDE BERNARD

able from the circumstances of the delivery of the lectures and of their publication. The more important of the topics dwelt upon in these several courses of lectures have been referred to in their proper place in the preceding chapters. It may, however, be worth while to point out the especial value of the lectures on animal heat, not only in that they contain, as we have already indicated, an exposition of Bernard's views as to influences of nerves on the chemical changes of the tissues and so on the development of heat, but also and perhaps especially in that they embody the results of his observations on the topography of bodily temperature, on the differences of temperature presented by different organs and parts, and on the causes of those differences. For Bernard largely extended, or perhaps rather established, our knowledge of this subject.

HIS LATER WRITINGS

In the long bibliographical list of Bernard's writings, a break is found in the year 1863. While from 1843 onward, each year is marked by some and generally by many utterances, he published nothing between the fall of 1862 and the spring of 1864 ; in 1863 he was wholly silent. The incessant labours of the preceding years had told upon him ; and in the winter of 1862-63 he wholly broke down. The state of his health gave great anxiety to his friends, they feared that the brilliant inquirer was prematurely to be taken away from them. The exact nature of the malady which attacked him was in many ways obscure. It was an abdominal affection, apparently an abscess, giving rise to periodical attacks of fever and acute pain, with intervening remissions. An exact diagnosis was never made, but it seems not unlikely that the illness

CLAUDE BERNARD

would nowadays have been recognised as appendicitis. He suffered from it at intervals until 1866-67, when, after a most severe attack, accompanied by intense fever, during which his life was despaired of, the abscess appears to have discharged into the bowel. He then slowly recovered his health, and by 1869-70 had become once more sound and strong.

The early attacks of the malady led him in 1862-63 to desert his laboratory and seek for restoration to health by a long sojourn in his ancestral home at St. Julien. The rural abode with its surrounding vineyards had not passed into other hands. Bernard, since the death of his parents, had kept possession of it, and thither he had been wont to return each autumn, restoring his mind and body during his vacations with the pure air of the country and the quiet occupations of a rural proprietor.

HIS LATER WRITINGS

Here, in the soothing autumn days, he went to and fro, tending his garden, caring for his fruit trees, many of which had been grafted by his own hands, and above all watching over the vintage, the produce of which appeared upon his table at Paris.

In this quiet retreat he spent the greater part of the year 1863; but as health and vigour came back, at least in part, to him, the daily round of rural pleasures and occupations soon began to be too small to fill his mind. Away from his laboratory and instruments, experimental inquiry was impossible for him; but the science of his adoption was ever present to his mind, and he made use of this enforced leisure and his returning vigour to develope in a systematic manner those views on the nature of the true methods of physiological

CLAUDE BERNARD

inquiry, which from the very first had guided him in his investigations, and of which he had from time to time, as occasion presented, given out fragmentary utterances. The result was a volume, published in 1865, entitled "Introduction to the Study of Experimental Medicine," and intended to serve as the introduction to a larger work with the title " Principles of Experimental Medicine ;" this latter however never saw the light.

In this " Introduction " Bernard expounded that conception of biological inquiry to which he gave the name of " determinism." When he began his medical studies he found, as we have already said, the opinion very common—his teacher Magendie himself holding it—that really vital phenomena were not subject to law, and therefore were beyond the pale of scientific investigation by experiment

HIS LATER WRITINGS

and observation, this being applicable only to the "physical phenomena of life." Bernard's position was that the manifestations of the properties of living bodies are bound up with the existence of certain physico-chemical phenomena, and that the latter furnish the conditions of the former. He insisted that in living, no less than in non-living bodies, natural phenomena are rigorously dependent on conditions, and that in the case of both the object of scientific inquiry is to lay bare the connection of the phenomena with the conditions. He expressed himself somewhat as follows:
"In both biological and chemico-physical studies the inquirer meets with a double set of conditions. He has to consider, on the one hand, the body in which the phenomena occur, and, on the other hand, the external circumstances, or the 'medium' by which the manifestations of the pheno-

CLAUDE BERNARD

mena are determined or provoked. In both studies the rigorous determination of the conditions is possible because matter itself is devoid of spontaneity, in both studies the limits of our knowledge are the same, in both studies in order to arrive at the 'determinism' of the phenomena, it is necessary to bring those phenomena into experimental conditions as definite and as simple as possible. The experimental physiologist knows nothing either of spiritualism or of materialism ; such words belong to an effete philosophy. We do not know and never shall know either spirit or matter. First causes do not belong to the domain of science; they will ever be beyond our grasp, whether we are dealing with living or with non-living things. The true experimental method has no, part whatever in the chimerical search of the ' vital principle ; ' there is no more a vital force

HIS LATER WRITINGS

than there is a mineral force, or, if one prefers to say so, the one exists quite as much as the other."

To push forward a vigorous and exact analysis by physical and chemical means of the phenomena of living bodies, was Bernard's conception of the task of the physiologist, the analysis being carried out either by simple observation or that "provoked observation" which is called an experiment. This led him, in the work in question, to caustic remarks on systems and doctrines. "Experimental medicine, that is physiology, belongs to no medical doctrine and to no philosophic system."

It is worthy of note that in his various writings Bernard repeatedly uses the phrase "experimental medicine" as identical with "physiology." To his mind it was perfectly clear that the treatment of disease was simply the practical application of pathological truths; and it was equally clear that all distinctions between pathology and physiology, as those between health and disease, were artificial, or of the surface only. To him the phenomena of the living body presented the same fundamental features, and had to be studied by the same canons of inquiry, whether the body in which they appeared were called sick or called sound. But, though he never doubted in the progressive power to solve the problems of disease of a growing physiology, which increasingly laid hold of the deeper and more general laws of life, he saw the dangers which beset the premature application to practical needs of unripe and superficial physiological views. He says at p. 348 of the work of which we are speaking—

"But no one in the present state of biological science can pretend that physiology

HIS LATER WRITINGS

is able to supply complete solutions of pathological problems; we must ever strive to solve those problems by physiological inquiries, for that is the true scientific path ; but we must carefully guard against the illusion that we have already gained the solution. Hence, the prudent and reasonable course at the present moment is to explain all that part of disease which can be explained by physiology, and to leave that which we cannot so explain to be explained by the future progress of biologic science. This kind of successive analysis, which, in its application to pathological phenomena is carried only so far as the progress of physiological science permits, isolates little by little, by way of elimination as it were, the essential element of the disease which is thus being studied, lays hold of its characters with greater exactitude, and allows therapeutic efforts to be directed

CLAUDE BERNARD

with greater certainty. Besides, with progressive analytic advance, the proper character and physiognomy of the disease are preserved. But if, instead of this, some delusive approach of physiology and pathology gives rise to the ambition to explain prematurely at one step the whole of the disease, then one loses sight of the patient, one gets a wrong idea of the disease, and by a false application of physiology, experimental medicine is hindered instead of being assisted in its progress."

No less clear than his views of the relation of physiology to medicine were his conceptions of the philosophical aspects of physiology. In many popular writings may often be found the idea that the progress of the experimental sciences, such as physiology, is the result of a combination of the labours of two kinds of men. In such writings it is taught that the new

HIS LATER WRITINGS

facts of science are gathered in by a laborious set of men who make experiments and observations, and thus bring to light new things; but who, humble in nature, and lacking the power of insight into deep truths, leave the truths thus discovered to be dealt with by higher minds, who, relieved from the tedious labour of collecting facts, can spend all their energy in the elaboration of great generalisations. The former are, in the eyes of the popular writers of whom we are speaking, men of science in the general acceptation of that term; such men are happily abundant. The latter, much more rare in their occurrence, are spoken of as philosophers. The former are mere labourers, delving after little truths; the latter hold the lamp which lights the others to their work. The writers in question point to Francis Bacon as such a philosopher, such a holder

CLAUDE BERNARD

of the lamp, and seem to think that to the light shed by him, the great advancement of natural knowledge which marked his time, and the times which followed, was mainly due.

Such was not Bernard's view. He says, " men of science, as Maistre has said, make their discoveries, work out their theories, and build up their science, without the aid of philosophers. They who have made the most discoveries in science are those who have never known Bacon ; and those who have read him and meditated upon him have, like Bacon himself, had but little success as inquirers."

It may be added that no one who has any knowledge of the development of sciences will do otherwise than agree with Bernard as against the popular writers. Indeed, the characteristic trait of scientific inquiry, in whatever branch, is, that it is

HIS LATER WRITINGS

even in its humblest efforts " philosophy." Moreover, not only is it well-nigh impossible to reach the solution of even the smallest scientific problem without finding that it bears on some truth greater than itself; but it is also, and even more so, impossible to gain a true insight into larger scientific verities without a strict and often a prolonged apprenticeship, in what to the popular writer seems the hodman's part of scientific inquiry. Only by letting the spirit which dwells in each branch of science soak, as it were, in the mind by repeated and almost daily converse with its facts and simpler truths, can any one hope to get a real grasp of its higher teachings.

The meditations on method to which Bernard was thus led in his enforced retirement, though they were merely the fuller development of what had been

CLAUDE BERNARD

in his mind from earlier days, made themselves felt during the whole of the rest of his life. Even in his earliest papers, short as they often were, he frequently turned aside from the narration of an experiment, and the discussion of the conclusions which might be drawn from it, to point a moral as to the excellence of this or that method, and to insist on the criteria of the true spirit of inquiry. But from this time onward deliverances on method became, in all his writings, longer and more frequent. Indeed, it may almost be said that the rest of his life was in the main devoted to the completion of his earlier labours, and to an exposition, richly illustrated by instances new as well as old, of the principles which ought to guide the investigator into biologic problems. Though never a year was passed, though never a course of lectures, or even

HIS LATER WRITINGS

a single lecture, was delivered without his bringing to light some new fact, or placing some old fact in a new light, he never again made known results of such supreme importance as those which his earlier labours had brought to him. He was led more and more into general views, and the problems which he attacked in his lectures took on more and more a general nature.

These features may be observed in the contribution which he made in 1867 to the "Recueil des Rapports sur les progrès des lettres et des sciences en France," and which was republished in 1872 under the title of "De la Physiologie générale." They may also be seen in his various later lectures. But they are conspicuous in his "Leçons sur les phénomènes de la vie communs aux animaux et aux végétaux." Indeed, in his later days he became more and more drawn towards those fundamental properties of living bodies which may be observed alike in animals and in plants.

In this latter line of inquiry he was a leader. Every inquirer, it is true, into physiological problems who, whether in these latter days or in the old times, has reached the truth in some special investigation, has looked with wistful eyes at the deeper, more general, questions which lie below the special ones, and which are, as it were, laid bare by the solution of the special problem. Those general questions are such that in discussing them the superficial differences between the plant and the animal seem of insignificant moment. To-day, perhaps, when so many special problems have been successfully solved, men's minds are becoming more than ever busied with such general problems presented

HIS LATER WRITINGS

by all living beings, whether simple or complex, whether called animals or plants. And Bernard, in being drawn especially towards such problems, was a pioneer on a line of inquiry which is now engaging many active minds, and which seems likely. to be energetically pursued, and to bear fruit even in the near future.

VIII

LATTER YEARS

IN the summer of 1864, soon after his return with at least temporarily restored health to active life and the joys of laboratory work he made his first acquaintance with the Court. In his private life he had ever shown a retiring disposition; nothing could be more repugnant to his nature than any wish to push himself into the notice of those whom others might consider as great and influential. He had his own idea of what true greatness was; he knew, too, his own worth; and he only cared to be thought well of by those of whom he himself thought much. He felt honoured when the great men of mind praised him, and counted it a great thing when the Academy took him into its select fold. But he had no desire for, and indeed shrank from, social distinctions and from marks of favour at the hands of those in high places. Had he wished otherwise, the way would have been easy for him. With Duruy, now high in political position, he had been familiar while the politician was as yet a humble professor. With Henry St. Claire Deville, who at that time was on terms of intimacy with the Emperor, he had close personal relations, being indeed much attached to him. These, or others, could readily have brought him into the circles of high society. For a long time, however, he held aloof. Not that he had any very

CLAUDE BERNARD

strong political feelings, but he simply did not care for social distinctions. One day, however, the Emperor Louis Napoleon, always anxious to secure the goodwill of eminent men of science, invited Bernard to take part in the festivities at Compiègne. Bernard accepted and paid the visit in company with Pasteur, who was also one of the many invited guests. The Emperor, as is well known, had pronounced spiritualistic tendencies; and it may be readily imagined that when he began to talk with Bernard he found he had come across a mind able to tell many things which were to him of a new and startling nature. So fascinated was he with what the physiologist had to say concerning the problems of life and the proper attitude of mind in which to approach them, that the talk instead of being limited to a few courtly remarks and polite rejoinders, was

LATTER YEARS

prolonged, to the envy of others, into a lively discussion of some two hours' length, which the Emperor concluded by saying, "You are a great man of science, and I want you to be pleased with me." Calling to his side M. Duruy, the then Minister of Public Instruction, he said to him, "You know M. Claude Bernard; see that he has all that he wants."

A few days afterwards the Minister sent for Bernard, and asked him what could be done for him. "For myself," said Bernard, "I want nothing; but my science is in great want of proper laboratories." Up to that time his only laboratory had been the one at the Collége de France, for the chair which had been created for him at the Sorbonne carried with it neither laboratory nor assistant. As the result of the interview at Compiègne two well installed laboratories were established, one

CLAUDE BERNARD

at the Sorbonne, the other at the Museum d'Histoire Naturelle at the Jardin des Plantes, the latter in connection with a chair of Physiologie générale, which was being instituted for him there, and into which he entered in 1868, relinquishing the chair at the Sorbonne to his pupil, Paul Bert.

Thenceforward his life, though it continued to be one of labour, was one of well-being and honour. In 1868 he was admitted into the Académie Française, and made one of the "Immortals," replacing Flourens; he took his seat on May 29th in that year, pronouncing, according to custom, the Éloge on his predecessor.

In 1869 the Emperor made him a Member of the Senate; but he never took his seat, and the events of 1870 deprived him of it. He had conquered the Emperor, but the Emperor had also conquered

LATTER YEARS

him ; and though in earlier days he might have been considered as an Orleanist, not so much from personal conviction as because many of his early associates belonged to that party, he at this time might have reckoned among the Imperialists. For this reason, perhaps, but also and perhaps still more because he felt no real interest in such things, he held aloof for the rest of his life from politics, though he became friends with many of the men of the Republic, more especially with Gambetta.

During these latter days he lived in comparative comfort, in adequate apartments on the first floor of No. 40, Rue des Écoles, just opposite the chief entrance of the Collége de France. He had by this time quite recovered from the illness of which we spoke in the last chapter. Indeed his health had become better than it ever had been before ; from being thin, worn, and pale, he grew to be somewhat stout, and a healthy colour was to be seen in his cheeks. He lived alone, for the dissensions with his wife, to which we referred some time back, had led to an early separation, and his two daughters, his only children, were also estranged from him. One of these, who is, or a short time ago was, still alive, was so far removed from sympathy with her father's labours, that she spent much of the means which fell to her in founding hospitals for dogs and cats, with the view of atoning for what she considered the crimes of vivisection which her parent had committed. He lived alone, attended by an old servant maid, who, devoted to him, and a skilful cook, took all possible care of him, so far at least as was consistent with the fervent performance of her religious duties. When on Sunday afternoons she was away at vespers, he had himself to open the door to any one who called; and, on one occasion, somewhat displeased at having to do this, petulantly said to his visitor, "It is not for the sake of 'le Bon Dieu' that Marie has gone out. These vespers serve as an opera to servant maids."

He went very little into society, visiting only at a few houses, for the hours which he spared from the laboratory were fully occupied with various labours. Besides the two lectures, which at least he gave weekly, he was very constant in performing his duties towards the societies to which he belonged, the Académie des Sciences, the Académie de Médecine, and the Société de Biologie.

Yet had he pleased, he might have been much sought for. He had charmed the Emperor, and indeed he charmed every

CLAUDE BERNARD

one who had the good fortune to meet him. Tall in stature, with a fine presence, with a noble head, the eyes full at once of thought and of kindness, he drew the look of observers on him wherever he appeared. As he walked in the streets passers by might be heard to say, "I wonder who that is; he must be some distinguished man."

And his talk was brilliant, when he was moved to speak. Scattered through his lectures may be found many pithy and epigrammatic sayings; and many others fell from him in friendly intercourse. When one day he said to Gambetta, "It is that which we do know which is the great hindrance to our learning that which we do not know"—the acute politician declared it was even more true in politics than in science.

In his later years his closest personal

LATTER YEARS

friends were perhaps Berthelot, the chemist, and Renan, the philosopher, both his colleagues at the Collége de France ; their friendship was one of some thirty years' length ; and very often at the close of the day's work the three met in Bernard's laboratory and held together a brief, but genial and witty talk, to the great delight of the young assistants present. He was also very intimate with Davaine, and followed with great interest that inquirer's first bacteriological investigations ; indeed he at a very early epoch grasped the great importance and significance of microbic life, and he watched the development of Pasteur's great researches with an attention and appreciation born of a clear insight into their surpassing value.

In his early days he was much attached to the distinguished physician and pathologist, Rayer, whose influence over him at that time was perhaps second only to that of Magendie, and who was of great help to him in his early struggles. Towards his old master, Magendie, his affectionate attitude was almost that of a son, so soon as he had overcome the initial dislike which the former's rough nature and abrupt manners had engendered. Though as his own intellectual character grew he could not help seeing more and more clearly Magendie's failings as a scientific inquirer, he as it were shut his eyes to much; in many respects he followed the lead of his master with almost the obedience of a child. He was especially influenced by Magendie's opinion of the worth of various workers in science. An investigator whom Magendie held in light esteem, or denounced as a mistaken opponent, Bernard made no effort to draw near to; and hence in early days he kept

LATTER YEARS

aloof from many men, from Poiseuille, for instance, to know whom would have been of great advantage to him. Indeed it was not until long after Magendie's death that Bernard wholly freed himself from his old master's influence.

As for his pupils, these simply worshipped him. Some great men in spite of their intellectual force, in spite also of the possession of a wholly upright and open character never succeed in gathering round them a body of young men, bound by the ties of personal attachment. Such men are masters in their writings only, not in themselves ; the bonds between them and their pupils are of the incorporeal intellectual kind, and have nothing of that body which is fed by love of and esteem for the man. It was not so with Bernard. He had, it is true, pupils in all countries, pupils who had never seen his face and who called him

CLAUDE BERNARD

master only because they knew the worth of what he had done. But over and above these he had a closer band of personal pupils, not men of Paris or of France only, but of other lands as well, who had heard his voice, and had watched his hand in the laboratory, and who knew him as a man no less than as a scientific worker. All these loved, admired, and indeed venerated him, not only for the great things which he had done in science, not only for his quick intellect and for the wide grasp of his mind, but also, and perhaps no less, for his charming character and his moral worth.

In 1877, the last year of his life, Bernard made three contributions to the Société de Biologie. One in April was on his old theme, Animal Heat; in this he advanced nothing very new, but dwelt on the topography of the temperature of the blood,

LATTER YEARS

and on the view that heat was produced not in one special seat, but in all the tissues, in proportion to the chemical changes of nutrition taking place in them. Once more, also, and for the last time, he insisted on the difference between thermic and vaso-motor nerves. A second in May, and a third in June, were both on gastric juice; thus in these he again returned to the subject of his earliest researches. He also contributed three papers to the Académie des Sciences : one on May 7, a second on May 28th, and a third on September 10th, all three dealing with the old subject of the glycogenic function of the liver. The first is a mere brief note, accompanying the presentation to the Academy of his Leçons sur le Diabète ; in this he remarks on the importance of studying pathology, from a physiological point of view. The second and third

CLAUDE BERNARD

constitute a more elaborate exposition of his views of the glycogenic function of the liver, during life and after death. He maintains that the latter is simply the continuation of the former, and concludes with the pregnant observation that, while the mechanism of the production of sugar out of starch and out of glycogen, by means of a ferment, is completely parallel in animals and in plants, the question whether a like parallelism holds good with regard to the formation of starch and of glycogen, yet remains to be seen. This is a problem with which he is occupied, and he trusts before long to have something to say about it. That something, alas! was never said.

The last course of lectures which he delivered was one at the Collége de France during the last months of 1877, the subject chosen by him being the tech-

LATTER YEARS

nique of physiological experimentation. It was an extended and developed repetition of a course which he had given years before, in 1859-60, at the same place. He recognised himself how much of his success as an investigator had been due to his manual dexterity. He further recognised that this was no accidental condition; on the contrary, he saw that the exact and vigorous analysis of physiological phenomena was in the highest degree dependent on operative skill. Two things, he insisted, were needed for a successful physiological experiment: a clear idea suggesting the experiment, and skill to put the idea to the adequate test. As he said in his "Introduction à l'étude de la médecine expérimentale" (p. 8): "To be worthy of the name, the experimentalist must be at the same time theoretical and practical. He ought, on the one hand, to be completely master of the art of establishing the experimental facts which serve as the materials of science, and, on the other hand, to have a firm grasp of the scientific principles which guide our reasoning in the midst of the widely varied results of the experimental study of natural phenomena. You cannot separate these two things, the head and the hand. A dexterous hand without a head to guide it is a blind tool. A head without a hand to realise its wishes, is an impotent nothing."

In the many lectures which he had given, with the exception of the course just referred to, and in the numerous memoirs which he had written, though he had never failed to give from time to time directions about the hand, he had dwelt chiefly on the head and its ideas. This last course of lectures he proposed to devote entirely to the hand. Nothing he felt was too

LATTER YEARS

small, too humble, too insignificant to leave unnoticed. He knew only too well that the success of an experiment might turn on what seemed to be the merest trifle. And he laid out for himself the task of embodying the vast experience of his life in the fullest and minutest exposition of the details of physiological experimentation as it ought to be carried out in order to ensure the greatest result. Thus in the course of lectures in question, after spending some time on the exposition of general considerations, he descends to the lowest details of the laboratory, beginning with precise instructions as to the handling of an animal and as to the administration of anæsthetics in preparation for an experiment.

The course was published after Bernard's death, under the title of "Leçons de Physiologie opératoire." But, alas, only

CLAUDE BERNARD

the first five of the lectures were revised by Bernard himself, the last on his very death-bed.

Drawn in his latter days, as we said, more and more to ponder over the fundamental properties of living matter, his mind dwelling more and more on the phenomena which are common to all living things, whether animals or plants, he could not but be led to meditate often on the changes in living beings brought about by the actions of so-called ferments. These he had come across in his very earliest researches. They had been present to him in this research or that, during his whole life ; and while he had been making France famous by the discoveries on which we have dwelt in former chapters, his friend and colleague, the illustrious Pasteur, had been adding like increments to that fame by his researches on alcoholic fermentation.

LATTER YEARS

As is well known, Pasteur had come to the conclusion that while some changes, often spoken of as those of fermentation, such as the conversion of starch into sugar, can be carried out by means of the so-called soluble, unorganised ferments or enzymes, the change of sugar into alcohol and carbonic dioxide is the direct act of the living yeast cell, needs the immediate intervention of a vital factor, and is therefore by its very nature wholly removed from the category of ordinary chemical reactions. As is also well known, he explained this special vital action involved in the formation of alcohol, as a contrivance on the part of the cell to obtain for its ordinary processes of nutrition a supply of oxygen under circumstances in which no supply of free oxygen was present in the medium in which it was living.

CLAUDE BERNARD

To Bernard this calling on the cell as a *Deus ex machinâ* to serve as an explanation of what could not otherwise be explained, was in flagrant discord with the principles of biological inquiry on which he had again and again insisted ; and, though his great friendship with Pasteur probably led him to abstain from open criticism, he seems to have marked the problem as one towards the solution of which experimental inquiry might be directed. In 1876 he had said in a letter : "I have in my head ideas which I must above all things work out ; " and this possibly was one.

At all events during his holiday stay at St. Julien, in the autumn of 1877, he made a large number of experiments on the fermentation of the juice of the grape. On his return to Paris he continued these experiments in his laboratory during

LATTER YEARS

November and December. But he said little about them, no one had a very clear conception of what were the ideas which he was putting to the test, and as we shall presently state, a fatal illness brought the inquiry to a premature end. While prostrated on what was to prove his death-bed, he said one day to his pupil d'Arsonval, "I believe that I have obtained some results which will put alcoholic fermentation in a wholly new light; but I am too tired and weak at this moment to explain them to you." The strength and clearness of mind needed for the explanation never, alas, came back to him, and whatever views he might have had went down with him into the grave. The thought that he was not to live to give to the world the full exposition and convincing proof of his conception saddened his dying hours. " It would," said he, "have been grand to have ended with that."

After his death, when his effects in the cottage at St. Julien were being examined, a number of very rough and brief notes were found hidden away, and these seemed to indicate the line on which he had been working. They were certainly not in a condition fit for publication; and it is perhaps to be regretted that the enthusiasm of his pupils led to their appearing with an explanatory note in the " Revue Scientifique," on the ground that nothing which the great master had written, however incomplete it might be, ought to be lost.

The publication of these notes gave pain to Pasteur, who saw that their effect was to destroy the theory on which he had insisted so much; he could not bring himself to believe that his old friend who was

LATTER YEARS

always wont to exchange ideas with him most fully and freely, could have thus been so long working so to speak against him, without saying so much as a word of what was in his mind. And some words on the matter passed between Pasteur and Berthelot in the Académie des Sciences.

It would be unjust to lay any great stress on these rough notes of a set of experiments obviously tentative and incomplete, or, from abrupt sentences written down here and there, to infer that Bernard thought that he had solved his problem. Still it seems very clear that he did think that he was at least on the road to the proof that alcoholic fermentation could be carried out by means of a soluble ferment, working outside the cell, and so apart from any direct action of the cell, a ferment capable of performing its task amid the free access of oxygen.

CLAUDE BERNARD

Had he lived to complete this inquiry of his, Bernard would, by some twenty years, have anticipated Buchner, his successor in this line of inquiry; his very last research, fragmentary as it was, was a parting proof of how far ahead the light of his genius threw its rays.

During November and December of 1877, Bernard was busy in his laboratory at the Collége de France, chiefly occupied with these fermentation experiments; but on the last day of the year he was seized in the laboratory with a chill, and left it to return to it no more. The chill marked the onset of a grave illness, an acute affection of the kidneys. After lingering for some time he finally passed away on the 10th of February, 1878.

Even on what was to prove to be his death-bed he could not be wholly idle.

LATTER YEARS

The lectures on "Physiologie opératoire," to which we referred above, as being delivered at the Collége de France during the preceding winter and spring, were being prepared for publication by his pupil, Mathias Duval ; and Bernard strove to the end to give these a final revision before they saw the light. But only the proofs of the first five lectures thus felt the touch of the master's dying hand ; his strength then failed him, he could do no more. The last words which came to the public from him who had wrested such great truths from Nature by experimental inquiry, were words devoted to counsel as to those minute details of the conduct of a physiological experiment, by which the fruitfulness or barrenness of the experiment is so much determined.

At his death all Paris wept. In the

CLAUDE BERNARD

Chamber of Deputies the then Minister of Public Instruction, M. Bardoux, proposed that the great man whom France had just lost should be laid in his grave with all the pomp and ceremony of a public funeral, at the expense of the State. Gambetta, acting on the occasion as the Reporter of the Budget Commission, supported the proposal in a speech in which, speaking not only as an admirer but as a friend, he dwelt on the greatness and goodness of the man who had passed away, insisting that, among other marks of an exalted mind, he possessed this great one, that he had never let himself be led away, either by party spirit or by the dogmas of a school or by private feelings. Up to this time France had given such a token of national esteem to none but princes, statesmen, or soldiers. Bernard was the first man of science or of letters who was thus laid to rest with the

LATTER YEARS

display of a great procession and a solemn function in the draped cathedral of Notre Dame.

Dumas, Vulpian, P. Bert, Moreau, and others spoke at the grave in the name of the several societies and institutions with which Bernard had been connected. A year later, in February, 1879, Paul Bert, who followed Bernard in the chair at the Sorbonne, and was, perhaps, his favourite pupil, delivered a discourse upon him in a Conference at the Sorbonne ; and a little later, in April, Renan, in succeeding Bernard at the Académie Française, pronounced his Éloge.

In 1886, a bronze statue was erected to him in the court of the Collége de France, the seat of his so many brilliant labours ; and in 1894 another statue was erected at Lyons, in the great court of the Faculty of Medicine and Science.

IX

CONCLUSION

IN the preceding pages we have attempted to show what Claude Bernard did for Physiology, and to indicate, in some detail, the workings of his mind by which he was led to lay hold of the truths which he lay bare to mankind. If we go a step further and attempt to analyse his genius, if we put to ourselves the question what were the qualities of Bernard's mind and character (for the two cannot be separated in an investigator), by which he stood above the barren or even the ordinary industrious inquirer, by virtue

CONCLUSION

of which he, instead of groping long and wearily in dimness if not in darkness, as it were, rapidly or even suddenly diving into the obscure, brought out the truth at once into light, we shall find three conspicuous traits. I say nothing of his conscientious adherence to exact truth, of his refusing to think he saw that which might be expected to appear but was not to be seen, of his never being willing to look upon the " almost" or " very near " as good as " quite." This he had in common with many other observers whose results have nevertheless been of mediocre value. And without this he too, in spite of all else he had, would have been barren or worse. But, over and above this essential condition of all successful inquiry, he had other prerogatives which are not often found in one man. Of these perhaps the most important was an imagination ever on the alert. In this respect he presented a strong contrast to his master Magendie, whose way was somewhat that of a prospector, prodding and digging in all directions, in the hope that the precious ore of a new truth might at times be turned up. Bernard, on the contrary, always worked under the guidance of some leading idea. "He," said he, one day, "who does not know what he is looking for, will not lay hold of what he has found when he gets it." And his fertile mind was ever ready to supply him with a clear idea by which to work. He has himself in his "Introduction à l'étude de la Médecine Expérimentale," given us an admirable description of the genesis and growth of a successful experimental inquiry. To the observer brooding over the phenomena presenting themselves to him there comes the thought that if a certain state of things were supposed to exist, or if a certain se-

CONCLUSION

quence of events were supposed to take place, the occurrence of the phenomena must necessarily follow ; and he forthwith set about to seek for evidence whether the things so supposed do really exist or no. Observation starts a hypothesis, and experiment tests whether the hypothesis be true or no. Such is a research reduced to its simplest terms. The experiment once devised must be carried out in accordance with acknowledged rules and precepts ; there is little or no scope here for differences in intellectual power between one inquirer and another. But in the origin of the hypothesis out of the observation, and in the framing of the needed experiment, there is room for all the difference between genius and stupidity or foolishness. It is in the putting forth the hypothesis that the true man of science shows the creative power

CLAUDE BERNARD

which makes him and the poet brothers. His must be a sensitive soul, ready to vibrate to Nature's touches. Before the dull eye of the ordinary mind facts pass one after the other in long procession, but pass without effect, awakening nothing. In the eye of a man of genius, be he poet or man of science, the same facts light up an illumination, in the one of beauty, in the other of truth; each possesses a responsive imagination. Such had Bernard, and the responses which in his youth found expression in verses, in his maturer and trained mind took on the form of scientific hypotheses.

An hypothesis may be good or may be bad, may be fruitful or may be barren. This may, on the one hand, depend on the very nature of the hypothesis, which may, even at the outset, in its very origin, be worthless and wrong. On the other

CONCLUSION

hand, failure or success may depend on the framing of the experiment by which the hypothesis is tested. Here, too, the imagination comes into play. The man who constructs a hypothesis without supplying an adequate programme for its trial by experiment, is a burden to science and to the world; and he who puts forward hypotheses, which by their very nature can not be so tried, is worse, for he is a purveyor of rubbish. We can never know what rejected ideas passed through Bernard's mind, ideas rejected so soon as born, because they were unfitted for trial; probably to his as to other like fertile minds, there came many thoughts which he buried at their birth, letting live only those which seemed to him of promise. But this we may say that the force of his imagination was as conspicuous in the framing of experiments to test his views as in the quick-

CLAUDE BERNARD

ness with which new views sprang up in his mind.

In the framing of experiments but not in the carrying of them out. In this we may recognise a salient difference between the foolish and the wise investigator, between the false scientaster and the true inquirer. In the case of the former, imagination, even though, as sometimes happens, it may have been dull and sluggish in building up the hypothesis and planning the experiment, awakens into riotous activity while the experiment is going on; it sees visions and dreams dreams; it sees in the results of the experiment things which never were, is blind to things which stare it in the face, and comes away with a distorted and lying picture of what has taken place. In the case of the latter, imagination, knowing that its work is done so soon as the experiment begins,

CONCLUSION

stands aloof during the whole time that it is going on, making way for calm, frigid observation which, in its perfect action, while it lets nothing escape it, sees nothing but what really is. Such was Bernard's way when he came to the experiment which his imaginings had prompted. Active before and after the experiment, during the experiment itself his imagination was, as it were, dead.

Another conspicuous trait of Bernard, on which we have already dwelt, also the product of his quick imagination, was the readiness with which he turned aside from an inquiry on which he was already engaged, to follow out a new line of inquiry suggested by some intercurrent fact. To divine when thus to turn aside and when not to turn aside but to go straight on, regardless of side issues however tempting, is perhaps the chiefest sign of genius in inquiry. The man who, refusing to take heed of any beckoning by the way, plods doggedly on along the path which he has marked out for himself, may miss a golden opportunity. On the other hand, the man who is always ready to leave the main track in order to follow out the bye-paths, which in almost every inquiry open out from time to time on either hand, runs the risk of losing his way in blind alleys and of coming late to his real goal, or it may be never reaching it at all. Bernard, in nearly every one of his inquiries, was led to turn aside from the road which, at starting, he had marked out for himself; his instinct guided him to leave the road at the right turning, and to follow a bye-path which brought him to a great result.

Lastly, Bernard's success was in no little measure due to his remarkable manual

CONCLUSION

dexterity. His hand was promptly obedient to his mind. His facility enabled him to put sharply and clearly the question which an experiment embodied ; and hence the answer came to him sharp and clear. His old pupils still speak with admiration of the almost marvellous celerity and directness with which he would perform a most intricate and difficult operative experiment. Without haste and without hesitation, taking step after step swiftly and in due order, he would with exact strokes lay bare and isolate a delicate structure by disentangling it, with the utmost neatness, from its perplexing surroundings, and would complete a difficult operation in time needed by others for mere preliminary preparation. It is told of him that sometimes, urged by the pressing need to get an immediate answer to some question with which his mind was stirred, he would come suddenly

CLAUDE BERNARD

into the laboratory, call for an animal, and then and there, without so much as removing his hat, perform an experiment, it may be, of no little difficulty. A false worship of intellectual supremacy has led some to ignore the value of bodily attributes as aids in the pursuit of truth, and as elements in the composition of genius ; and indeed in some branches of learning a failing eyesight and a clumsy hand do not present themselves as serious obstacles to success in reaching the inner secrets of the nature of things. In experimental science it is otherwise. Here great truths are for the most part come to by treading a flight of steps, each step an experiment resting on the one below, and leading to the one above. If any one step goes wrong the whole ascent is stopped ; and the experiment will go wrong if there be bungling in the execution of it, if

CONCLUSION

the details, even the minutest ones, fail to be deftly carried out. The clumsy experimenter may count himself fortunate if his clumsiness only leads to loss of time, if, through lack of the needed dexterity, he simply fails to carry out the experiment exactly as he wished, and therefore has to try it all over again. The much more common occurrence is that the want of skill mars the experiment, by introducing something, which enters unnoticed into the result and leads, without the experimenter being aware of it, to a wrong or imperfect answer being given to the question asked. A clumsy experiment is in most cases a bad experiment, leading to a wrong conclusion; and the evil which the clumsiness thus entails is all the greater, the more acute and the more active the mind which is guiding the clumsy hand. Hence it comes about that in experimental science

CLAUDE BERNARD

skilfulness of the hand, no less than quickness of the mind, must be counted among the attributes the possession of which gives a man the power to pierce swiftly and surely into the secrets of nature, the power which his fellow men seeing in him, speak of him as having genius. Such a skilled hand had Claude Bernard.

INDEX

A

Académie des Sciences, 57, 64, 74, 84, 94, 95, 108, 110, 114, 120, 141, 143, 150, 211
Alcoholic fermentation, experiments on, 219
Animal heat, influence of the nervous system on, 105
"Arthur de Bretagne," historic drama, 8

B

Barreswil, 48, 72, 74
Bell, Charles, 38
Bernard, Claude : birth, 1 ; childhood, 3 ; Jesuit College at Villefranche, 4 ; student at Lyons, 4 ; pharmaceutical assistant at Lyons, 5 ; literary aspirations, 6 ; writes vaudeville comedy, 7 ; writes prose drama, 7 ; starts for Paris, 8 ; "Arthur de Bretagne," 8 ; St. Marc Girardin advises him to study medicine, 9 ; medical studies, 9 ; life in the Quartier Latin, 10 ; first experiments on living animals, 13 ; opens an experimental laboratory, 13 ; appointed *interne* to Magendie, 16 ; official *préparateur* at the Collége de France, 21 ; beginning of his career as a physiologist, 21 ; strikes out a path for himself, 41 ; delivers private courses

INDEX

of lectures, 43; publication of first communication on chorda tympani, 44; dexterity in dissection, 45, 234; thesis for the degree of doctor of medicine, 45; experiments on gastric juice, 46; investigations on the spinal accessory nerve, 48; "Concours pour l'agrégation," 48; researches on the properties of the pancreas, 50; awarded the prize of Experimental Physiology, 57; researches on "recurrent sensibility," 58; researches on the production of sugar in the body, 66; the liver and the production of sugar, 71, 84; thesis for doctorate in Science, 76; discovers that puncture of the fourth ventricle causes temporary diabetes, 76; Glycogen, 85; "Internal Secretion," 91; "Bernard's granules," 94; further papers on glycogen, 95; "Leçons sur le Diabète," 96; discovery of the vaso-motor system, 100; influence of the nervous system on animal heat, 105; division of the sympathetic nerve, 106; researches on glandular secretion, 120; "Leçons sur la chaleur animale," 125; vivisectional experiment, 131; work on inhibition, 137; study of poisons, 139; curare, 140; carbonic monoxide gas, 149; spontaneous generation controversy, 158; difficulties of his early surroundings, 161; escape of dog with cannula and encounter with police commissioner, 165; appointed Magendie's deputy at the Collége de France, 169; un-

INDEX

satisfactory domestic relations, 170; first lecture as Deputy, 171; appointed to the new chair of general physiology, 173; elected into the Academy of Medicine and Surgery, 173; appointed full Professor at the Collége de France, 173; his enormous activity, 173; his lectures, 174; publication of "Leçons de physiologie expérimentale," 177; "Leçons sur les effets des substances toxiques et médicamenteuses," 177; "Leçons sur la physiologie et la pathologie du système nerveux," 178; "Leçons sur les propriétés physiologiques et les altérations pathologiques des liquides de l'organisme," 178; his later writings, 179; a break in his work, 181; his state of health, 181 : retires to the country, 182; "experimental medicine," 184; views on philosophers and men of science, 190; his first acquaintance with the Court, 198; is invited to Compiègne, 200; asks for new laboratories, 201; is admitted to the Académie Française, 202; created Senator, 202; chair of Natural History at the Jardin des Plantes, 202; relinquishes chair at Sorbonne to Paul Bert, 202; his attitude in regard to politics, 203; his daughters, 204 : personal appearance, 206; conversation, 206; personal friends, 206; influence of Magendie on him, 208; worshipped by his pupils, 209; contributions to the Société de Biologie, 210; last course of lectures, 212; the qualities of an

INDEX

experimentalist, 213; "Leçons de physiologie opératoire, 215; holiday at St. Julien, 218; experiments on fermentation of grape juice, 218; views on alcoholic fermentation, 219; last illness and death, 222; mourned by all Paris, 223; public funeral, 224; bronze statue erected at Collége de France, 225; another statue at Lyons, 225; analysis of his genius, 226; his methods of research, 228; value of the skilled hand in experimental science, 236

"Bernard's granules," 94
Berthelot, 18, 208
Bidder, 26
Bichat, 31
Blondlot and artificial gastric fistula, 55
Bois, Jacques du, 17
Boussingault, 64
Bowman, William, 29
Brachet, 110

Brown-Séquard and section of the cervical part of the sympathetic, 112
Budge, 110, 115

C

Carbonic monoxide gas, analysis of, 149
Cervical sympathetic, experiments on, 111
Chorda tympani, paper on, 44
Collége de France, 16, 44, 117, 143, 169, 173, 174, 177, 178, 212
Curare an arrow poison, 140
Cuvier, 18, 31

D

Dextrose, 68
Diabetes, researches on, 67; lectures on, 97
Dieffenbach, 166
Doctorate in Science, thesis for, 76
Drama, Bernard's historic, 8
Dumas, 64
Dupuy, 110

INDEX

E

Experimental medicine, 184

F

Facial paralysis, reference to, 47
Fattening of cattle, researches of Dumas, Boussingault, and Payen on, 64
Ferrous sulphate and potassium ferrocyanide, simultaneous injection of, 46
Flourens, 36
Fontana, 30

G

Gastric juice, thesis on, 45
Germany, dominant spirit of physiological inquiry in, 27
Girardin, Saint-Marc, 8, 9
Glandular secretion, 120
Glycogen, 61, 85
Gmelin, 53
Goodsir, John, 29

Grape juice, experiments of fermentation of, 218
Guidi, Guido, 17
Gundlach, experiments by, 64

H

Henle, 26, 104
Hensen isolates glycogen, 85
Hoppe (Hoppe-Seyler), spectroscopic observations on absorption of oxygen by the blood, 154

I

Imagination, value of, in experimental research, 80
" Internal secretion," 91

K

Kölliker, 105, 147
Kühne, Willie, microscopical search after glycogen, 93

L

Laënnec, 19
Lavoisier, 151

INDEX

Lehmann, 81
Liebig, 27, 64
Liver and sugar production, 71
Longet, 36
Ludwig, 120

M

Magendie, 16, 36, 58, 171, 172, 173
Magnus, 152
Marshall Hall, 28
Matteuci, 30
Meyer, L., 153
Müller, Johannes, 23, 102

N

Nerves, vaso-motor, discovery of, 100
Nervous system, influence of, on animal heat, 105

P

Pancreatic juice, inquiries into action of, 55
Payen, 64
Pelouze, 166
Petit, Pourfour de, 109

Philosophers and men of science, 190
Physiological science before Bernard, 22
Physiology at outset of Bernard's career, in Germany, 22; in England, 28; in Italy, 29; in France, 30
Poisons, experiments with, 140
Potassium ferrocyanide and ferrous sulphate, simultaneous injection of, 47

Q

Quartier Latin, life in, 10

R

"Recurrent sensibility," 58
Reid, John, researches on the cranial nerve, 28; on the vaso-motor nerve, 110
"Rose du Rhône," 7

S

Schwann, Theodore, 26
Sharpey, Professor, 28

INDEX

Société de Biologie, 52, 76, 85, 107, 115, 121, 138, 141, 210
—— Philomathique, 52, 59
Spallanzani, 30
Spontaneous generation, 158
Stokes, spectroscopic observations on the absorption of oxygen by the blood, 154
Sugar, researches on the physiology of, 66
Sylvius, Jacobus, 18

T

Tiedemann, 26, 53

V

Vagus nerve, experiments on, 137
Valentin and the action of pancreatic juice, 54
Vaso-motor nerves, discovery of, 100
Vidius, Vidus 17
Vierordt, 26
"Vitalism," 96
Volkmann, 26

W

Waller, 110, 114
Weber, E. H., 26

BIBLIOBAZAAR
The essential book market!

Did you know that you can get any of our titles in our trademark **EasyRead**™ print format? **EasyRead**™ provides readers with a larger than average typeface, for a reading experience that's easier on the eyes.

Did you know that we have an ever-growing collection of books in many languages?

Order online:
www.bibliobazaar.com

Or to exclusively browse our **EasyRead**™ collection:
www.bibliogrande.com

At BiblioBazaar, we aim to make knowledge more accessible by making thousands of titles available to you – quickly and affordably.

Contact us:
BiblioBazaar
PO Box 21206
Charleston, SC 29413

Lightning Source UK Ltd.
Milton Keynes UK
30 January 2010

149368UK00006B/10/A